THE CAMPUS CLERGYMAN

THE
CAMPUS
CLERGYMAN

PHILLIP E. HAMMOND

Foreword by
KENNETH W. UNDERWOOD

BASIC BOOKS, INC., PUBLISHERS
New York · London

To my parents

FOREWORD

The occupations and professions of our society, such as the clergy, medicine, and law, have provided our major models of the relations of commitment, theory, and technical skill to social action. They are now the scenes of searching and anxious reappraisal of their purpose and form for our time. The leaders of this reappraisal should welcome the increasing attention by social scientists, historians, psychologists, theologians, and others to the way in which particular world views or faiths are expressed in the occupational or professional structures of our major institutions and how reorientation toward life and work takes place in a rapidly changing world. This book in the sociology of occupation probes these basic realities both by choosing the clergy on campus as its object of study and by choosing a method of inquiry which draws upon classical theoretical concerns of its discipline and the more recent technical resources of empirical social survey.

The object of this study, the Protestant ministries in American higher education, has become for many churchmen a symbol of a necessary break from traditional parish ministries. For them, the campus ministry is concerned about serving the people absorbed in the work of one of the most influential institutions of our society, concerned about rethinking critically and openly the meaning of historic symbols of Christian faith, and concerned about creating new religious institutions if necessary to elicit the attention and respect of educated leadership in contemporary society. Certainly no other clergy in recent decades have been given greater freedom to live and work with students and faculty who are attempting to understand the modern world through a variety of disciplines and perspectives, to prepare for technical and professional careers, and to discover a meaningful, personal style of life.

For other churchmen, however, the campus ministry has become a symbol of radical, irresponsible repudiation of the images and structures by which the historic faith is made known, an adaptation of Christianity to secular ideologies (represented often by the social sciences). It has not been a new model of pastoral concern or of significant reinterpretation of the meaning of the Gospel.

The sociological study this book represents was undertaken with deep awareness of this situation in the churches. However, Professor Hammond's study probably will receive greatest attention from the kind of leadership which is not accurately represented by either of these views. This study will be welcomed chiefly by those who, like Professor Hammond, have discerned that profoundly complex forces are involved in the developments of the clergy on campus, forces having to do with the mission and task of the whole church and the present significance of the historic traditions and divisions of Western religious institutions. What the author, as a sociologist, sees at once as the basic problem of the campus ministry is its inability to establish viable institutional alternatives to the traditional ones which its most influential members have rejected and which are expressive of its deepest theological convictions. The crisis is particularly manifest in its ambiguous and confused professional expectations and the poverty of the churches' provisions for its training and evaluation.

The need for objective, critical study of campus clergymen —the need to see what patterns of ministry have actually emerged and what factors and events influence their development—has increased in every denomination during the past decade. But the issues which this study raises with such rigor and particularity are also historic and central to the whole movement of Protestantism. For what has obviously not yet emerged for the Protestant movement is a theory of profession and calling which consciously opens up for the clergy the major, alternative types of social action in the modern world and how these are to be expressed and related in the varied careers of clergymen in their work with laity. The question of the nature of Christian vocation or calling, which became for the "founding fathers" of Protestantism the focus of its argument with Roman Catholicism, takes on new urgency and form in a study of campus ministers. How do various professional resources, theories, and skills become instruments of Christian faith, serviceable not only as the source of ultimate hope but also serviceable in meeting the needs of people in their particular situation?

Such questions are made more urgent and fruitful by the methods of study and the scholarly role of Professor Hammond. The study is elegantly restrained in doing and claiming only what the academic discipline of the author makes possible. It does not claim to answer the theological and moral questions of the occupation studied, for example, whether a man should be a Christian clergyman or what policies should dictate the church's response to university inquiries into its life. The study describes the differences between campus and parish clergy and explores the relation of these differences to the ministers' views of the organized church and of religious dissidence. The study, though it is concerned with objective structures which can be discerned alike by believer and non-believer, probes the world views and values of the professional actors studied. The basic types of ministry described, for example, have to do with differentiated and undifferentiated concepts of the purpose and role of the clergy. The data given here—that the clergy trained to minister to people in a special structure of the society, the university, generally tend more to a multidimensional view of their role than those orientated toward a general parish situation—break many popular stereotypes of the ministry and raise serious questions for seminary and denominational administrative leaders. Professor Hammond does not presume to tell them what they must do, but he raises crucial policy questions.

The basic concern of this study, I should judge, however, is not to raise policy questions for the churches but to advance the knowledge and epistemology of sociology in an increasingly important area of specialization. *The Campus Clergyman* exemplifies a sociology of a younger generation of men who have transformed the debates between general theorists and radical empiricists. The former were willing to incorporate the realities of motivation and world view into their abstract models but unable to verify the operational and empirical implications of their work. And the latter were not concerned to probe, through their instruments of survey and statistics, the relationship of religious belief and commitment to social action.

Some of us may wish that this study went further in its attention to the theological aspects of the occupation studied or to the tensions between personal and collective styles of thought and action. Others of us may discern, in the campus ministerial role, identities and interpersonal relationships in institutions which are more varied and flexible, more tolerant of social tensions and ambiguous striving, more cognitively subtle and elaborate than that discernible by the discipline and instrument of this study. Such feelings and intuitions may be indicative of important realities, but it will take the fullest possible use of many resources of the university and the church—social services, psychology, history, theology, and the like—to reflect them in research and literature. Campus ministries may well be the most fruitful and manageable point in Protestantism for intensive, multidisciplinary studies of the clergy, just because of their exposed position between church and university.

Professor Hammond's book anticipates a series of studies of the campus ministry, studies being made from a variety of university disciplines and perspectives, all part of a process of policy considerations by key religious and educational leaders. This series is the Danforth Foundation Study of Campus Ministries. Professor Hammond's study was begun, it is true, before the Danforth inquiry was commissioned, but the writing of this book was supported by the Danforth study. Its conclusions, therefore, enhance the importance of the series, just as the series yet to be published will enhance, I believe, the significance of this book.

The Campus Clergyman, then, is a book which advances the work of sociology. But, in addition, it advances the work of those in university and church who wish to see the energies and imagination of their institutions directed to new knowledge and understanding of the nature of work in the modern world and to its placement in the liberating context of wider and deeper loyalties and powers.

KENNETH W. UNDERWOOD

Wesleyan University
February 1966

PREFACE

Why should an occupation, after more than a half-century, still look like a new endeavor? Why, after several generations of practitioners and many generations of clients, should it be unable to define its task clearly or hold on to its recruits firmly? Add the fact that many persons wish there were less ambiguity in the occupation and that it had a lower personnel turnover, and we are confronted with a puzzle. That puzzle —its nature, causes, and consequences—is the subject of this book.

The occupation in question is the Protestant campus ministry, in 1963 a collection of about 1,300 full-time persons, whose mission is somehow to articulate religion and higher education, the church and the university. Given its small size, and its rather tangential position in the world of work, one may wonder why this book has been written. The answer is twofold. From a theoretical standpoint, very little is known of infant areas of social structure. As Burton R. Clark noted in his *Adult Education in Transition:*

> Some action patterns are much more firmly established, widely prized, and deeply valued than others, and it is usually the well-institutionalized configurations that are denoted by the customary definitions and descriptions in sociology. But the analysis of institutional development needs to be concerned with nascent and immature forms.

The "nascent and immature forms" of the campus ministry thus make it a worthy object of study.

Second, despite the ambiguity and turnover, the campus ministry shows no sign of dying out. Indeed, it has been growing steadily since its inception. Furthermore, unlike blacksmiths or whaling men, whose "products" no longer fit the times, clergy on campus are not phasing out because the materials of their occupation are no longer relevant. The phenomenal growth of higher education itself—the continued increase in faculty, students, and variety of educational policies—means that religion's cause in higher education is far from moribund. And so seminarians continue to aspire to a campus ministry, colleges continue to add chaplaincies, and denominations continue to increase their budgets and bureaucratic apparatus.

But so also does the campus ministry continue in a state of ambiguity and high turnover. Hence this book.

Perhaps to write any book is to be overbold. But to write one about an occupation one has never practiced, or with which one has had little intimate contact, may seem downright presumptuous. The practitioner of an activity, it is true, will always understand more of its individual nuance than will the outsider. In this sense, his knowledge is always greater. But insofar as his knowledge is personal or based on the experiences he and his intimates have had, it may be incomplete. The individual nuance is his, but the *pattern* of nuances may be more readily seen by one who has access to systematic observation. This book is based on a study of the entire Protestant campus ministry, and therefore socially structured patterns emerge which cannot possibly be seen by informal glances, however insightful. Failure to understand this point will lead to disappointment upon reading the following analysis. For it is not an essay on how to conduct a campus ministry; it is not a treatise on "effectiveness"; and it is not an advocacy of one method over another. In those areas, the writer unhesitatingly bows to the expertise that comes with experience. But the present work is not so much about campus ministers as it is about campus ministry. The social structural patterns are highlighted; the individual nuance, therefore, is not.

If the reader expects to find advice, admonition, or advocacy in this book, he may be inclined to overextend H. Richard Niebuhr's point that

> if educational questions cannot be answered theologically, neither can theological questions be answered by use of the techniques of social or behavioral sciences, however relevant the insights derived from these sciences may be to theology.

First of all, "techniques" are merely techniques; by themselves they answer nothing. Eyeballs, like cameras, are blind, Norwood Hanson reminds us. But second, and more importantly, is it true that only theological questions can be asked about the campus ministry? It is, after all, an occupation. It has workers, places of work, means of support, methods, and even "products." Might not the concepts (not the techniques) of social science be relevant to—that is, be able to answer questions about—these aspects of the campus ministry? This book is predicated on an affirmative response, but its analysis is therefore limited to questions drawn from that range and to answers equally limited in scope. As a sociological analysis, its sole aim is to explain in structural terms the present state of an occupation—the campus ministry.

I was led to discover the sociologically interesting case of the campus clergy through chance discussion with Yoshio Fukuyama, and the National Institutes of Health (Grant M-6179) provided funds for the initial stages of investigation. By the time data were collected and analyzed, I was indebted to a number of students and colleagues. Yale University underwrote some of the costs of printing the questionnaire, and the Danforth Study of Campus Ministries, through the cooperation of its Director, Kenneth W. Underwood, and Robert Rankin, Associate Director of the Danforth Foundation, has been generous throughout, even to the point of providing me with a year off from teaching in order to complete the analysis. That year was spent at the Survey Research Center, University of California, Berkeley, through the courtesy of its Director, Charles Y. Glock, though my debt to him extends back to 1956, when I was first his student. Facilities at the Pacific School of Religion were also available through the kindness of Charles McCoy.

In addition to the cooperation I received from denominational officials, and of course the great majority of campus clergy, I should like to acknowledge the help of Richard F. Curtis, J. Edward Dirks, and N. J. Demerath III. Kenneth Underwood has become a valued friend; my debt to him, though it includes the Foreword to this volume, does not end there.

PHILLIP E. HAMMOND

University of Wisconsin
May 1966

CONTENTS

THE CAMPUS CLERGYMAN

PART I

1

THE DEVELOPMENT
OF AN OCCUPATION—
AND A PROBLEM

Does the college or university assume an obligation to improve its students' understanding of religion just as it assumes the obligation of improving secular understanding? If so, how might this be done? Do churches forfeit support when their members enter college? If so, what strategy might the church use? Who is responsible for seeing whether the pieces of a fractionized college education can be reassembled?

Out of issues like these has emerged a class of people whose vocation it is to bridge religion and higher education. Located in the college, they are spokesmen for the church. Most of them are ordained, but they typically serve no parish. They are committed to the idea of higher education, but their justification presumes shortcomings in the academic community. These people are campus ministers, and their occupation is the subject of this book.

THE CREATION OF A MINISTRY
TO HIGHER EDUCATION

The first university chaplain was appointed in the eighteenth century, and many schools demonstrated their religious ties through such practices as the appointment of clergymen as presidents and daily convocations. But the campus ministry as a distinctive occupation is chiefly a phenomenon of this century. Several colleges had chaplains before 1900; student Christian Associations (sometimes with adult leaders) were fairly common; and there existed isolated instances of denominational efforts to create student worship centers. But it was at the turn of the century that churches fully recognized that: (1) with expanding curricula, religion was no longer a part of every student's training, (2) with expanding faculties, ordained teachers were no longer common, and (3) with expanding college enrollments, especially in land-grant schools, a significant number of parishioners were students living away from the home church. New modes of ministering to colleges were therefore needed, and so began the campus ministry. It took two forms, the college chaplain and the university pastor.[1]

"The decade of 1900–1910 was one of local experimentation."[2] For example, Presbyterians recommended in 1904 "the appointment of special ministers who shall . . . care for Presbyterian students in state universities, very much after the pattern of army and navy chaplains."[3] In the same year Congregationalists expressed the desire that in each state university there be "a wise, able, tactful religious teacher who shall be a true pastor to the hundreds of young people belonging to our own field."[4] Baptists, Methodists, Lutherans, and Episcopalians also recognized the potentialities of this specialized ministry, and by the 1920s Southern Baptists and Southern Presbyterians had also evolved patterns of university work.[5]

Though denominations differed in how they conducted their campus ministries (and still do), the fact is that, from *ad hoc* arrangements in 1900, most of the major Protestant denominations had created in a quarter-century a pattern of activity involving adult leaders, student groups, buildings, intercollegiate associations, and even some interdenominational cooperation.

If churches were reasonably quick to see the possibilities of a specialized ministry, colleges also were interested. One of the results was their espousal of the chaplaincy. From 14 such Protestant positions in 1900, the number grew to 69 by 1942, and in the four years following the Second World War, 80 new chaplaincies were created.[6] Further positions continue to be added. There are now approximately 1,300 full-time or nearly full-time Protestant campus clergymen, of whom about one-fourth are chaplains.[7]

DIFFERENCES BETWEEN UNIVERSITY PASTORS AND CHAPLAINS

The chaplaincy and the university pastorate differ in a number of ways, most of which are related to the fact that the former is a "school" position whereas the latter is a "denominational" position. Chaplains, for example, are overwhelmingly in private or church-related schools; only a very few public institutions employ them. University pastors, on the other hand, are found more often at schools with larger enrollments—the public universities.

All but two chaplains in this study (99 per cent) report their base of operations to be an office in a college building. By contrast, only 16 per cent of university pastors have such an office, most of them instead operating from a denominationally owned or rented building on the campus periphery or from a local church. Similarly, 93 per cent of chaplains are "primarily responsible to or dependent upon" the college administration for planning their program, whereas the comparable figure for university pastors is 2 per cent. The latter are typically responsible rather to the denomination directly, to one of its administrative units (for example, diocese, district, local church), or to a local board of governors made up of clergymen, laymen, and faculty.

Generally speaking, chaplains have far greater responsibility to the college and, correlatively, more rights and privileges. The proportion of chaplains with a telephone listing in the college directory, for instance, is 93 per cent; for university pastors, 69 per cent. When asked if they have a regular channel to the college administration, 98 per cent of chaplains replied yes; by contrast, only 64 per cent of university pastors gave that answer. Respondents were asked how often, if ever, they were called in by the college administration "to give help or advice on policy matters, disciplinary measures, or the like." Half the chaplains reported they are "frequently" called in, and 35 per cent more are called in "occasionally." Only 4 per cent are "never" called in. By contrast, fully a third of the university pastors are "never" called in, almost another third are called in "rarely," and a mere 6 per cent are "frequently" asked to give help or advice to the administration.

The practitioners of the two types of campus ministry reveal other differences. For example, when asked "Do you have more contact with students of your own denomination than with other students?" 78 per cent of those in the university pastorate said yes, while only 24 per cent of chaplains gave that reply. Being chaplain to a total student body obviously alters the nature of student contacts; whether he desires it or not, the university pastor's clientele is more restricted.

The extent to which the two types of campus minister maintain certain ties with their denominations is seen in answers to two other questions. One question inquired how often respondents have contact, formal or informal, with *parish* clergy. Whereas 42 per cent of university pastors report such contact more than weekly, only half this proportion of chaplains do. And when asked if they have ministerial duties other than those connected with college or university people, half again as many university pastors as chaplains said yes (23 per cent vs. 16 per cent).

It is clear from just these few indications that in some respects there are at least two "campus ministries." Chaplains, on the one hand, are not only employed by a school to conduct a ministry but also have closer ties in many ways to the location of that ministry. University pastors, in addition to being employed by a denomination (or several denominations), are also more tenuously connected to their campuses. In terms of locus of responsibility and relationships with others, then, one can speak of two different campus ministerial positions.

THE MANDATE OF THE CAMPUS MINISTRY

In at least one important sense, however, one may correctly speak of a single campus ministry: The chaplaincy and the university pastorate share a distinctive mission, a single mandate. Each denomination states this mandate more or less clearly, and each campus minister more or less recognizes it. Thus:

> . . . the stated purpose of the United Presbyterian campus ministry is: "to bear living witness to the gospel of Jesus Christ . . . so that there will result a fellowship of faculty and students . . . [thus demonstrating] the credibility of the Christian position . . . making clear the evangelical Christian world view." [8]

It is the aim of the Christian ministry in higher education to nurture the Christian fellowship on the campus and to confront the academic community in the totality of its life with the

Christian faith and to lead its members to a commitment to God as revealed in Jesus Christ.[9]

Because of the Gospel, the campus Christian group is called upon to bear its missionary and prophetic witness to the Christian in the university, the Church, and the world. To this end ... The Methodist Church establishes campus units to study, worship, and work, in order to fulfill its mission of fostering a campus Christian community.[10]

These three statements reflect the formal aims of every Protestant denomination with an organized campus ministry. Each identifies the clientele (the university community), the message to be imparted (the Gospel), and the desired outcome (the community's commitment, leading to Christian fellowship).

THE CHANGING PHILOSOPHY UNDERLYING THE MANDATE

The mandate is shared, but the philosophy governing how that mandate is best carried out differs. Here the variation is *within* the chaplaincy and university pastorate, however, not between them. The variation is also found within each denomination. It can be likened to the changing philosophy of overseas missionary work:

The missionary movement is no longer an outreach of an established civilization into "heathen" lands. It is no longer an attempt on our part to reproduce our types and forms of Christianity among other people. It is no longer *our* attempt through *our* missionaries to carry on *our* work in distant lands.[11]

The concept of missionary, says Lamott, has changed from its first stage, in which the missionary is an Explorer, through a second stage, in which he is a Colonial Administrator, into the third stage, in which he is a Fellow Citizen.[12]

Some regard the campus minister as a "Colonial Administrator," a missionary sent by denominations to care for the well-being and faith of their student members,[13] while others vigorously oppose this view. The mission is *"within* the academic rather than *to* the academic community. . . . [It must] involve the whole campus . . . faculty and staff members as well as members of the student body." [14] The task is to "lead from the middle." [15] In other words, the campus minister, according to this view, should be a Fellow Citizen.

It is probably correct to say that most administrators in the "higher education" offices of the various denominations, many of whom are themselves experienced campus ministers, hold to the Fellow Citizen philosophy. In a tape-recorded interview, one of them told the writer:

> We are less impressed by what a campus minister does visibly in the way of activities than by what he does through the work of Christians on the campus and the work of the campus itself. Does he enable others to fulfill their tasks? The campus ministry used to be called student work—the projection of the mother image, a maternal concern for young people in one's own denomination. I find now when I talk with other denominations they basically agree that it's time we get beyond this denominational parental concern. The real issue is no longer one of facilities. The day was when students had no place to go for cokes, fireplaces, philosophies, and so forth. And denominations supplied what the university now does in its own buildings. Well, we're at the place where we recognize that a lot of the past doesn't work. We used to have reports once a year—how many students came out for this or that. No longer. Some people say guys can get awful lazy that way. It's true, they can. But we run that risk. Our ministry is to confront the university with the challenge of Christianity.

Another administrator says simply:

> One of the vital parts of the campus minister's work, as we see it, is to challenge the student's faith. And to challenge the university's faith, too.[16]

Like overseas missions, then, the campus ministry has undergone certain changes during its six decades of existence.
Though its mandate may be said to remain unchanged—it is
still a specialized ministry, located with a certain audience,
for the purpose of transmitting a specific message—the philosophy varies in just how this is best carried out. From a time
when secular education had few clergymen devoting attention to it, now most colleges with sizable enrollments have
at least one Protestant campus minister, and in some cases
there are more than a dozen. For this reason (and no doubt
many others), the nature of the enterprise reflects change.
Again, the missionary analogy is instructive:

> The existence of the church in all the major territorial divisions
> of the world changes the nature of our missionary responsibil-
> ity. . . . The function and work of the missionary thereby
> assume a new aspect. He goes out not as a supervisor or di-
> rector but as a fellow laborer, casting his life with national
> Christians in a common task.[17]

The newer point of view sees the campus minister casting his
life with the people of the academy, sharing their task, not
offering his in opposition.

AMBIGUITY AND TURNOVER IN THE CAMPUS MINISTRY

A program of Ping-pong tables and peanut-butter sand-
wiches coupled with Sunday-evening worship followed by
fellowship hours, though still very much in evidence, is therefore no longer the dominant Protestant approach to campus
work. At some schools, the best visiting lecturer series or the
most experimental theater can be found under the aegis of
the campus ministry. At other schools, the programs of social

action or of welfare service to surrounding neighborhoods are conducted out of the chaplain's office or the denominational foundations ringing the campus. At still other campuses, these foundations serve as open forums, allowing political and theological speakers who might otherwise be denied hearings.

But, though much of what it does is experimental, the campus ministry itself is no longer an experiment. The major denominations now have budgets, administrative apparatus, real estate, and conferences devoted to their ministry to higher education. Many seminaries are adding specialized training for the campus ministry. And professional journals and newsletters oriented to the practice of the campus ministry are beginning to appear. In one sense, it would be accurate to say that the occupation is "established."

With establishment has not come "stability," however. Despite its more than half-century of history and tradition, the campus ministry seems to be an occupation floundering in the uncertainties of its inception. Two indications of this stand out: First, its practitioners are highly ambiguous about the best ways to carry out their task; and second, there is surprisingly high turnover.

There can be no doubt that ambiguity is widely felt in the occupation. Each of the denominational officials interviewed mentioned it as one of his concerns, as did many of the campus clergymen. "Our denomination as well as all others are up against a very ambiguous situation," said one chaplain. "I think there is a very real ambiguity even in the role of the chaplain," said another. "You can never go in, as a parish minister does, and know what the objectives are that the church has laid down." "Our main complaint," stated a university pastor, "usually is that we lack definition or job description, or what it is we are expected to be doing."

These are not complaints expressed only in private to an

interviewer; campus ministers very readily make the charge in public.

> Neither professor nor preacher, neither group worker nor priest, neither psychiatric counselor nor student—but involved in all these roles;—what can we call the campus religious worker? [18]

And John Cantelon, in his inaugural sermon as Chaplain of the University of Southern California, warned his listeners (he did not need to warn himself) that "the chaplain must be preserved in a role that is necessarily ambiguous." [19]

Nor is this ambiguity a recent development. As early as 1911, the Congregationalists surveyed their ministry to 21 state university campuses and concluded, "on the basis of an extensive correspondence, that there was no consensus . . . among pastors in university towns as to the best program and that the solution must be left to practical experiment." [20] This long-felt and long-recognized problem is confirmed in the questionnaire data. At one point respondents were told: "Some observers have noted a lack of specificity in campus ministerial duties. They say that a man coming to a new position has little idea of what is expected of him, and that little agreement exists among others of what he is to do. In short, they say the campus ministry has a vague job description." Respondents were then asked, "How accurate a portrayal of *your position* is this observation?" They answered as shown in Table 1–1. And when asked further, "Do you agree with

TABLE 1–1.

Very accurate. My position is vaguely defined	17%
Quite accurate. My position is not very clearly defined	36
Not very accurate. My position is quite clearly defined	35
Inaccurate. My position is very clearly defined	12
	100%

this observation about the campus ministry *generally?*" fully 77 per cent agreed that "the observation is essentially correct." Over half claim their own positions are vague, and over three-fourths see vagueness as characteristic of the campus ministry. Moreover, in answer to another question 70 per cent agreed that "more specification and clarity" would be helpful.[21]

TURNOVER IN THE CAMPUS MINISTRY

It is perhaps natural that in the first years of an occupation the flow of personnel in and out will be high. The problems of establishing guidelines, making contacts, and the frequent necessity of having to invest considerable time before results begin to show—all these factors contribute, no doubt, to instability among first practitioners. The very intrepidity associated with "pioneers" probably signifies a reduced need for the security of tenure and steady career. We are not surprised if the first ones in may be quick to get out.

But after sixty years should there not be a reduction in turnover? After specialized training becomes available, professional associations are formed, and bureaucratic apparatus is created, do we not assume a greater stability in personnel? Certainly some denominational officials in the campus ministry think so. "I think we have more career men," said one in an interview. "I think the age is getting older and the stay is getting longer." "I think in the past there has been more temporariness," said another. And yet all the available evidence suggests quite the opposite. *The average age is younger now than before, the length of tenure is shorter, and the degree of commitment to remain in the campus ministry is less,* at least for university pastors, who comprise three-fourths of the occupation. That evidence can now be reviewed.

In keeping with "normal" expectations, the average amount of education of campus ministers has increased. Shedd reports that only 27 per cent of university pastors in 1931 had more than a B.D. degree.[22] In 1963, the comparable figure is 50 per cent. According to Smith, 57 per cent of chaplains in 1948 had more than a B.D. degree.[23] In 1963, this proportion had increased to 73 per cent. Clearly, campus ministers are better educated now. But instead of a comparable increase in average age, chaplains have changed but little, and university pastors are considerably younger.

Shedd reports that "in 1930, two-thirds of the university pastors felt definitely committed to [remain in] student work." [24] A question designed to elicit a comparable figure was asked the 1963 university pastors: "Is it your intention now to make the campus ministry your life-long vocation?" Only 15 per cent chose the answer "Yes, definitely," while another 34 per cent chose "Yes, probably." Even adding the "probables" to the "definites" results in a figure below the 1930 proportion who were then "definitely committed" to remain.

A second kind of evidence supports the explanation of higher turnover. Both Smith and Shedd provide the percentages of their samples who had, at the times of those investigations, served their positions for less than three years.[25] Identical data from 1963 indicate that though *fewer* chaplains today are new to their jobs (44 per cent in 1963 versus 67 per cent in 1948), *more* university pastors are new to theirs (60 per cent in 1963 versus 40 per cent in 1931). It would seem, by inference, that the turnover rate of chaplains has decreased over the years whereas that of university pastors has increased. Several qualifications are needed, however, which keep that inference tentative.

1. Because the data indicate how long persons have been in their positions, they may not reflect movement out of the campus ministry but only movement from given positions. We know from the present data, however, that most of those moving from a position move entirely out of campus work.

(This was true of four-fifths of the "movers" in a one-year span, 1963–64.) Unless this ratio of leaving entirely to leaving for a similar post has increased greatly since 1931 (which seems highly unlikely), then the *relative* difference between the two time periods is not incorrect, though the *absolute* turnover may be overestimated.

2. A second qualification concerns the possible confounding of results from the creation of new positions. This situation is unlikely, however, since the campus ministry has grown steadily from its beginning at the turn of the century. The more recent the time period investigated, then, the *lower*, not the *higher*, will be the proportion of newly created jobs.

In spite of the inferential nature of the evidence thus far, the turnover rates of chaplains and university pastors appear to have changed, the former's decreasing, the latter's increasing. Direct evidence, available for university pastors only, supports that proposition.

In 1938, Shedd reinvestigated the people who had been his respondents in 1930–31. He found that "sixty per cent of this group are in the same or similar student work positions." [26] This would mean (for the original cohort) an annual attrition rate of 5 per cent (100 per cent − 60 per cent = 40 per cent over eight years). As we shall now observe, the present annual attrition rate—chaplains as well as university pastors—is just about *triple* that figure.[27]

Campus Ministerial Turnover for One Year

The names and addresses of the campus ministers of eleven denominations plus the membership of the National Association of College and University Chaplains were taken in the spring of 1963 from the 1962–63 rosters of those organizations. The result was a list of 1,263 persons who thereby became the universe and sample of this study. One year later it was possible to check those names and addresses against the 1963–64 rosters and record whether each person: (1) remained in his post of a year before, (2) appeared not at that post but another one, or (3) disappeared from the campus ministry rosters altogether. (See Table 1–2.)

TABLE 1–2.

| Per Cent Who | Among Respondents | | Among Non-Respondents | All Campus Ministers |
	Chaplains	University Pastors		
Remained	86.4%	83.3%	78.1%	82.9%
Changed	1.2	4.2	1.9	3.1
Left	12.4	12.5	20.0	14.0
TOTAL	100.0%	100.0%	100.0%	100.0%
N =	(250)	(747)	(266)	(1,263)

The surprise here is not only that the turnover is high, but also that it is equally high for chaplains and university pastors. If the rate for this one year is at all typical, both types of campus ministry undergo the *equivalent* of a complete change of personnel almost every seven years.

Is this a high rate of turnover? The answer, of course, depends upon what one uses for comparison. Compared with the campus ministry in the decade of the 1930s, the campus ministry now appears to have high attrition. Even contrasted with the turnover in public-school teaching, an occupation notorious for its personnel changes, the campus ministry's rate of turnover is high.[28] Or compared with college admissions directors, whose entrance as an "adjunct" occupation into higher education coincides with that of "religion in higher education" and thus renders their profession apt for comparison, campus ministers have high turnover.[29]

The real test of whether turnover in an occupation is high, however, depends upon the standards desired by those concerned with the occupation. No one is surprised, for example, that college student bodies undergo complete changeover every four years or that the populations of hospital maternity wards change every few days. But church organizations and college officials do not select recruits for the campus ministry with the expectation that they will soon leave. The campus ministry is not designed to make leaving "natural" and staying "unnatural."

One church official, in charge of his denomination's college work, said in an interview: "Seminary students come to me and say, 'I'd like to enter the campus ministry before I go into parish work.' We discourage this greatly. It isn't a sort of stopping-off spot." Another official, recognizing the shift through the years in policy regarding the appropriate length of campus ministerial tenure, said: "There is still a feeling on the part of the whole church that it is nice to have some young man to minister to a campus for a couple of years before he goes into the real work of the church. I think many of our campus clergy have faced this feeling and gotten over it."

The official statements of philosophy and purpose of most denominations make it very clear that short-term service in the campus ministry is hopefully to be avoided. For example, the United Presbyterian Church, U.S.A., reports that several major policies have been adopted "to assure that well-qualified men will be challenged to enter the campus ministry, will have a long and satisfying service in it, and will find status and tenure comparable to that of other ministries of the church." [30]

The United Church of Christ, in a working paper of 1959, recommended that its campus ministers be provided with pension and social-security coverage, in-service training, and sabbaticals.[31] The Lutheran Church–Missouri Synod makes clear its preference in such statements as "A campus internship . . . is necessarily helpful for the person who intends to spend his life in campus work." [32] The Methodist Church, in a pamphlet on the chaplaincy, states that "there must be an increasing number of men who enter this work with a sense of deep dedication. Only thus will they be motivated to pay the high price of preparation or enabled to remain on the campus when attractive offers to go elsewhere are forthcoming." [33]

TURNOVER AND AMBIGUITY AND THEIR CORRELATES

The administrative dislike of shorter tenure may well be based on the knowledge that it can be related to ambiguity, and it is ambiguity which is unwanted. Certainly the association of these two has long been recognized. As early as 1938, one campus clergyman suggested "few clear-cut responsibilities, an amorphous job" as one reason for short-term campus ministers.[34] The Methodist Church, in a special report on its college chaplains, gives as a first reason for their rapid turnover: "Vague job analysis and/or administrative indecision regarding the actual duties of the chaplain." [35]

The data of the present study support this interpretation. The one-year attrition rate of those who report their own position to be "very vague" is two and one-half times the rate of those in "very clear" positions (20 per cent versus 8 per cent).[36] Correlatively, ambiguity is related to present intention to stay or leave the campus ministry. In answer to the question "Is it your intention now to make the campus ministry your life-long vocation?" slightly more than a third (36 per cent) of those in "very vague" positions responded with "Yes, definitely" or "Yes, probably." Two-thirds (67 per cent) of those in "very clear" positions now intend, definitely or probably, to stay. Without having to agree that turnover results *only* from ambiguity (there are, it should be remembered, occasional illnesses, ecclesiastical directives to move, even retirements, as well as more enticing positions which may contribute to a decision to leave), we can readily see that some sizable portion of campus ministers' lack of commitment to their occupation is attributable to its vagueness.

But the adverse effects of ambiguity are manifold. Those reporting their own positions to be vague are less likely to enjoy their work than those in clear positions (32 per cent versus 55 per cent agree with "I can't think of any work I'd enjoy as much") and more likely to perceive the majority of campus ministers as having low morale (50 per cent versus 23 per cent). They are less likely to report coming "quite close" to fulfilling their objectives in their ministry (19 per cent versus 43 per cent), less likely frequently to "feel a sense of accomplishment" in their work (47 per cent versus 72 per cent), and more likely frequently to "have doubts about" their work (30 per cent versus 7 per cent).

INSTITUTIONALIZATION OF THE CAMPUS MINISTRY

Occupations which are ambiguous and whose practitioners feel less than committed to remain in them can be said to be poorly institutionalized. Institutionalization in this sense is the degree to which positions are socially structured,[37] a process which typically is thought to consist of two empirically related but analytically distinct components. First is the question of how widely understood are the expectations relevant to the position, expectations held both by the occupants and by others who interact with occupants. Second is the degree to which these expectations are taken seriously, that is, the degree to which partners to the interaction are committed to the fulfillment of the expectations.

To assert that the campus ministry is poorly institutionalized, then, is to suggest that: (1) expectations of what the
campus minister shall do are not shared to any great degree,
and (2) commitment to whatever are the expectations is not
great, including the expectation that the campus ministry is,
or should be, a long-term career. Ambiguity and low career
commitment are thus seen not only as causally related to each
other but as related indications that the campus ministry is
not yet institutionalized.[38] This is the focus of the present report—why is this the case?

Before beginning the answer to this question, however, we
must devote some further attention to the general phenomenon of institutionalization. Chapter 2, therefore, holds in
abeyance any direct discussion of the campus ministry, but
instead presents some conceptual apparatus for pursuing the
question. Chapter 3 then resumes the investigation of clergy
on campus.

NOTES

1. Nomenclature for college clergy varies. In this report, "chaplain" means (following the National Association of College
   and University Chaplains in their criterion for membership)
   "administratively employed and/or designated" by a college
   or university. All others are called here "university pastors."
   Differences between the two types are discussed below.
2. Clarence P. Shedd, *The Church Follows Its Students* (New
   Haven: Yale University Press, 1938), p. 14. This work and
   Seymour A. Smith, *The American College Chaplaincy* (New
   York: Association Press, 1954) and Merrimon Cuninggim,
   The College Seeks Religion (New Haven: Yale University
   Press, 1947), contain historical accounts of the American
   campus ministry.
3. Quoted in Shedd, *op. cit.*, p. 14.
4. Quoted in *ibid.*, p. 17.
5. *Ibid.*, pp. 22–28, 87.
6. Smith, *op. cit.*, pp. 8–14.

7. See Appendix for a description of the enumeration and location of this population, as well as a description of how the study was conducted.
8. From *The Campus Ministry*, prepared by the United Presbyterian Church, U.S.A. (n.d.), p. 33.
9. From Newsletter No. 61, Division of Higher Education, Congregational Christian Church, 1956.
10. From "The Philosophy of College and University Religious Work," The Methodist Church, 1957.
11. Willis C. Lamott, *Revolutions in Missions* (New York: Macmillan, 1954), pp. 21–22. (Italics in the original.)
12. *Ibid.*, pp. 28 ff. The early dominant expression of this changing philosophy was William E. Hocking, *Re-Thinking Missions: A Layman's Inquiry After One Hundred Years* (New York: Harper, 1932). There is now considerable reaction, calling for a return both in technique (e.g., D. A. McGavran, *How Churches Grow* [London: World Dominion Press, 1959]) and in theology (e.g., Stephen Neill, *Creative Tension* [London: Edinburgh House Press, 1959]).
13. The title of Shedd's 1938 report, *The Church Follows Its Students*, reflected this point of view. His subsequent work, however, does not.
14. D. R. Heiges, "The Church's Ministry on Campus," *International Journal of Religious Education*, XXXV (1958), 14.
15. J. S. Duley, "The Work of the Church in the University," *Christian Scholar*, XLII (1959), 22.
16. Two recently published accounts of the changing philosophy of the campus ministry are John E. Cantelon, *A Protestant Approach to the Campus Ministry* (Philadelphia: Westminster Press, 1964) and George L. Earnshaw, "A General Philosophy for a Relevant Campus Ministry," in Earnshaw (ed.), *The Campus Ministry* (Valley Forge: The Judson Press, 1964), pp. 17–35.
17. Lamott, *op. cit.*, pp. 2–3.
18. Harry Smith, "Between Two Worlds—The Role of the University Christian Worker," *The Christian Scholar*, XXXIX (1956), 209.
19. Delivered October 2, 1960. Other examples can be found in Duley, *op. cit.*, pp. 6–7, and Seymour Smith, *op. cit.*, p. 47.
20. Shedd, *op. cit.*, p. 45. The feeling of ambiguity apparently extends to Hillel (Jewish) Foundations. See R. L. Rubenstein,

"Religion and the Academic Community: The Creative Tensions of Faith and Learning," *Judaism: A Quarterly Journal*, VIII (1959), 142–151.

21. Nine per cent thought more flexibility is needed; 20 per cent were satisfied with present job descriptions; and 1 per cent failed to answer.

22. Shedd, *op. cit.*, p. 246.

23. Seymour Smith, *op. cit.*, p. 124. Both Shedd and Smith report very high response rates, comparable to the present study's.

24. Shedd, *op. cit.*, p. 272.

25. Seymour Smith, *op. cit.*, 122–123; Shedd, *op. cit.*, p. 272.

26. *Ibid.*, p. 272.

27. Actually these will not be comparable calculations since Shedd's annual rate is based only on an original cohort. Any persons entering the campus ministry after 1931 and leaving before 1938 would represent additional turnover but not appear in Shedd's computation. Inasmuch as we do not know how typical are the years involved anyway, these rates cannot be taken literally but only as evidence that the turnover has very likely increased.

28. W. S. Mason and R. K. Bain, *Teacher Turnover in the Public Schools, 1957–58*, U.S. Department of Health, Education, and Welfare (Washington: Government Printing Office, 1959), estimated annual attrition to be 11 per cent, and this includes many females for whom teaching is a temporary stop en route to homemaking.

29. A third of the admissions directors have been in their present positions for ten or more years whereas only 18 per cent of chaplains and 8 per cent of university pastors have been. See J. Hauser, *The College Admissions Officer*, report of the Bureau of Applied Social Research, Columbia University, 1964, p. IV–41.

30. *The Campus Ministry*, prepared by the United Presbyterian Church, U.S.A. (n.d.).

31. Available from the Division of Higher Education, United Church of Christ.

32. From a mimeographed document available from the Commission on College and University Work, The Lutheran Church–Missouri Synod (n.d.).

33. *The Methodist College Chaplain*, issued by the Board of Education, The Methodist Church, 1961, p. 10.

34. "Is the College Pastorate a Permanent Profession?" *Religious Education*, XXXIII (1938), 37.
35. *The Methodist College Chaplain*, p. 9. The annual turnover of their chaplains estimated by Methodists in this report, incidentally, is 25 to 30 per cent.
36. Turnover among those in "quite vague" positions is 13 per cent; in "quite clear" positions, 9 per cent. Even though the remaining figures in this chapter are cited only for extreme categories, this step-by-step relationship applies to them as well.
37. The phrase "in this sense" is doubly important in this context since the literature in Protestant churches typically uses "institutional" in a different sense, frequently in a pejorative manner. The "institutional" church has, in some circles, come to mean the encrusted, unyielding defender of the status quo. In other circles, "institutional" refers to the concrete organization in contrast with the ideals it represents, e.g., the Priesthood of Believers. Neither of these other meanings of "institutional" is implied here.
38. In other words, though in the short run ambiguity may lead to turnover, in the long run high turnover may contribute to continued ambiguity among successive generations of campus ministers.

2

THE PATH OF
INSTITUTIONALIZATION

Institutionalized patterns of activity imply the substitutability of persons but the non-substitutability of expectations. That is to say, if a pattern of behavior is sufficiently "set," then various persons may enter, learn, and conform to the expectations, and leave the arena without noticeably altering its normative structure. Similarly, attempts to alter the normative structure will meet with resistance. This, of course, is not to deny that individuals may effect change or that change may in fact occur. But an "institution" is not simply the creation of the persons who happen to be active in it now, nor is it infinitely malleable or malleable without consequences. An institution involves persons but is itself the amalgam of procedures they follow and uphold as right. A pattern of activity, to the degree it is institutionalized, is therefore marked by shared expectations and commitment to them.

When we ask, then, why a certain occupational role has failed to "set," to establish, to institutionalize, we are asking why the expectations governing that role's activities are insufficiently known and shared or, if known and shared, why they do not evoke commitment.[1] We are seeking for blockages, reasons which prevent expectations from becoming learned, shared, and internalized.

Four questions come to mind. Is there failure in recruitment —inappropriate persons are asked to perform the role? Is there failure in training—expectations are inadequately transmitted? Is there failure in motivation—commitment to the expectations is inadequate? Is there failure in adaptation—inadequate articulation exists with the social world surrounding the role? [2] Failure would be indicated by systematic or patterned irregularities at one or more of these points. A particular person, for example, may fail to understand the demands of a role because he, as a person, is peculiarly inept. Such a case would not indicate failure at institutionalization, however, unless: (a) the recruitment procedures regularly selected inept persons or (b) the training procedures regularly produced ineptness in recruits. Similarly, a particular individual may not be committed to fulfill the demands of a role because to do so would violate his own values. But, again, failure at institutionalization is not indicated unless: (a) the various demands "built in" to the role are themselves incompatible or (b) those demands are incompatible with the demands of other roles regularly held by the participants in the role in question. It is *patterned* extraordinariness, in other words, which is sought as the explanation for failure at institutionalization—situations where inadequate recruitment, training, motivation, or adaptation are themselves socially structured.

Conditions for Institutionalization: Some Illustrations

These four areas may be thought of as "conditions" which must be met if institutionalization is to proceed, and therefore as possible sources of blockage in the case of impeded institutionalization. Several illustrations will demonstrate the applicability of these notions.

It has been the observation of many travelers in developing nations, for example, that many of the white-collar bureaucratic and technological jobs in those countries are performed badly or performed not at all. Thus, ballots fail to get printed or fail to get distributed, and elections must be rescheduled. Airplanes are ordered, but airports are never built. Among the reasons advanced for these occurrences is the fact that the population simply does not contain enough persons with enough skill to perform these jobs. Similarly, in many welfare agencies in the United States, the positions of agent and client are only vaguely defined. The agent is uncertain whether he is to determine qualifications for welfare dole, engage in psychotherapy, or hand out money and advice. The client, on the other hand, is notorious for failing to keep appointments, save receipts and records, or spend his welfare money wisely. Again, part (though only part) of the failure is attributed to the inadequacy of the persons involved.[3] In both instances— of developing nations and of welfare agencies—one factor in the failure to institutionalize roles is recruitment; not enough people with the requisite skills are enlisted in the endeavor.[4] In the example of bureaucratic behavior in developing nations, this failure was noted in connection with the occupants of the positions in question; in the welfare agency, recruitment may be inadequate both to the position of agent and that of client (counterposition).[5]

A second condition for institutionalization is "training," the procedures whereby expectations come to be known and shared; failure therefore may be located in inadequate provision for developing and transmitting expectations. Goode suggests this is one of the problems of librarianship. "Librarians themselves have found it extremely difficult to define their professional role and the knowledge on which it rests. . . . The repeated calls which librarians have made for 'a philosophy of librarianship' essentially express the need to define what *is* the intellectual problem of the occupation." [6] Parsons attributes part of librarians' unclear identity to their diverse working conditions, that is, even should one sector of the occupation understand their tasks, other sectors may be unable to share in that understanding.[7] In this case, we see that the training condition is not met. It is assumed that persons recruited as librarians (as well as librarians' role-partners) have the capacity to perform a task; the problem is one of defining the task and training them to do it.

Suppose now a third type of situation, one in which the various persons involved are fully competent and clear about what to do. But they are not motivated to do it. Institutionalization is arrested in this case at the point of commitment. Clark supplies an illustration from his study of adult education. Not the administrators but "the public" (role-partners) lack motivation. Therefore, administrators have tried to "legitimize" their work by arguing that adult education is: (1) a low-cost operation, (2) a valuable public-relations instrument for the entire school system, and (3) an answer to a public demand. Thus, the administrators imply, their role-partners (taxpayers, school board, actual or potential adult students) *should* be committed to the fulfillment of the expectations.[8]

A fourth area of possible blockage remains to be illustrated. Suppose that role-occupants as well as their role-partners are capable, knowledgeable, and motivated to carry out their tasks. But because of the social location of one or both of these populations, conforming to these demands means automatic deviance from other demands. This is one of the classic instances of role conflict, or incompatibility of equally legitimate demands. The military chaplain provides an illustration. Recruited, trained, and motivated to perform certain activities, the military chaplain finds that the location of his work and therefore the nature of his relationship with clients make his performance difficult. Discussing how military chaplains confronted this dilemma, Burchard tells us:

> None of the respondents would of his own volition raise questions concerning the morality of killing, or of war in general, or of turning the other cheek, or any question concerning the relationship between religion and war. . . . [There is] the tendency to withdraw from it—to compartmentalize role behaviors and to refuse to recognize conflicting elements.[9]

Thus, the condition of adaptation was inadequately met.

The discussion to this point has been conducted as if barriers to institutionalization occur in isolation. This is clearly not the case in reality. By recasting the analyses of two patterns of activity—one involving impeded institutionalization, the other successful institutionalization—into the terms outlined above, we can demonstrate that the conditions of recruitment, training, motivation, and adaptation are inextricably bound together. Barriers to successful recruitment may lead to unsuccessful training, just as maladaptation may have consequences for motivation, to cite only two instances.

AN ILLUSTRATION OF
IMPEDED INSTITUTIONALIZATION

Burton R. Clark investigated public junior colleges in order to discover the sources of their "status, identity, and autonomy" problems.[10] Here was a pattern of activities, a set of roles, that had come into existence by "rational invention and intention." A need had been felt, and procedures to meet it had led to the creation of higher-education units called junior colleges. The result to date (at least for the school he looked at closely and thus, by implication, all public junior colleges), however, is "a school whose place in education is by no means clear and whose character has been problematic." [11] The junior-college system, one would say, is not fully institutionalized.

We cannot, of course, duplicate all of Clark's excellent analysis; for a full appreciation of all the factors impeding the institutionalization of junior colleges, one must turn to the report itself. However, several of those factors, repeated here, demonstrate how the conditions identified above are inadequately met. By simply noting with the symbols R, T, M, A, which of the conditions is involved, we can see that many concrete factors have multiple consequences:

(1) Some junior-college students simply cannot afford four years away from home and so enroll with the intention of transferring after one or two years in the home-town junior college (R). Many others, however, are not qualified to enter baccalaureate programs and thus are terminal students in junior colleges (R).

(2) There are, then, at least three possible "definitions" or programs for the junior college, each indicating different faculty, facilities, and budgets: a transfer student's curriculum, approximating the first two years of a four-year college; a terminal student's curriculum to introduce the liberal arts at a lower level; a terminal student's curriculum consisting of vocational education. Each of these programs implies different expectations regarding appropriate behavior for students, teachers, administrators, parents, alumni, and so forth (T).

(3) Faculty and administrators are recruited chiefly from secondary-school systems (R). Staff members recruited elsewhere (R), however, do not share the former's service orientation and belief in local control (T). So recruitment of staff as well as students creates confusion over whether the junior college is an extension of secondary school or a unit of higher education (T).

(4) Confusion over what is appropriate behavior for the various junior-college personnel (T) means disagreement over proper credentials for teachers (R).

(5) The various orientations toward junior college by staff and students (T), coupled with the various sources of person-

nel (R), make justification of one's task difficult (M). Teachers may not have a "conviction" that the less-qualified students properly belong in college (M), and student dropout is excessive (M). Conversely, one of the important functions of the junior college (the "cooling out" function, or helping students accept aspirations other than college graduation) is not compatible with teachers' values of inspiring students and helping them succeed (M). The result, says Clark, is "diffuseness of commitment" on the part of the junior college generally.

(6) Because the junior college is locally controlled by the city school system, it has little self-determination (A). Its vulnerability to local influences is seen in: its recruiting teachers from high schools in other districts rather than "raiding" its own (R); its suspicion of the "overtrained" teacher who will be concerned only with the superior, transfer students (R); and its acceptance of the "open-door" policy for student admission (R). The structural sources of low self-determination (A), therefore, have consequences for the nature of person brought into the milieu (R), for their mixture of expectations (T), and for their differing motivation to conform to those expectations (M).[12]

Alteration in any one of the areas of recruitment, training, motivation, and adaptation will be felt in the other areas. Successful institutionalization implies, then, at least some alignment of factors so that occurrences in one area do not undermine occurrences elsewhere. How these various areas can be in alignment can now be demonstrated with another example.

AN ILLUSTRATION OF SUCCESSFUL INSTITUTIONALIZATION

In his study of the U.S. Forest Service, Kaufman was struck by all of the factors that would seem to militate against "organization and unity."[13] The great distance, for example, between national and district headquarters and individual rangers, the ideology of decentralization, the variety of situations under the jurisdiction of the Forest Service from recreation to timber harvest to watershed to range use, and so forth, all suggest the difficulty of administering the Service. And yet, says Kaufman, the U.S. Forest Service has been notably successful; it has "vanquished the tendencies toward fragmentation." [14] It is highly institutionalized.

Again, by paraphrasing a number of explanations that Kaufman supplies, and noting by symbol the condition being met, we can see the interrelationship of recruitment, training, motivation, and adaptation:

(1) The Forest Service conducts recruitment campaigns and, despite rather stringent educational requirements, can select from an oversupply of applicants (R).

(2) Once accepted, however, recruits are given orientation courses, conferences, and on-the-job training (T). And there are seven volumes of the *Forest Service Manual*, plus a volume of directives for each region, plus the technical handbooks, to which rangers and their role-partners may refer for guidance (T).

(3) The "identification" of rangers with their jobs (M) is enhanced through the use of symbols (uniform and badge) and through headquarters' consultation with them. Public-relations work (for example, against forest fires) legitimates rangers' activities in the eyes of the public and "builds grass roots support" (M).

(4) Conflict-producing situations are minimized (A) by selecting persons in the first place (R) who demonstrate by their specialized education (T) their motivation to serve the Forest Service (M), by eliminating barriers to communication up and down lines of authority (A), by framing policy and handling outside groups through a central office (A), by rapid transfers so that rangers are not "captured" by local populations (A), and by frequent inspections (A).[15]

Because of Clark's and Kaufman's analyses, therefore, one can understand why the U.S. Forest Service has less trouble with "status, identity, and autonomy" problems, why its "place is clear and its character is not problematic," why—in short—it is more institutionalized than the junior college.

THE PATH OF INSTITUTIONALIZATION

Surrounding the phenomena of shared expectations and commitment to them are conditions of recruitment, training, motivation, and adaptation. If institutionalization is to be facilitated, there must be provision for meeting these four conditions.

But when are conditions "being met"? What, in other words, are the criteria for deciding the extent to which expectations are shared and commitment to them exists? Even a cursory look indicates that enacted occupational roles do not spring full-blown from nothing. Some steps must precede others; some features may be more strategic than others. If the end product may be a set of activities governed by shared expectations to which persons are committed, there must be a *path* by which this end product comes about.

Mills discovers something of this path in his research on a small group formed ostensibly for the purpose of studying "human relations" cases. The group began only with those expectations and commitments brought by individuals from elsewhere or imposed on it by the experimenter. Meeting regularly throughout an academic year, however, the group in time

> dropped certain preconceptions, displayed a range of possibilities, experienced progress in learning, intellectually and emotionally, and gained a sense of goal direction. . . . [Now its] central issue is to legislate an enabling set of norms . . . con-

cerning what should and should not be done, and concerning what sorts of interpersonal relations should prevail.[16]

This process Mills calls "negotiating an indigenous normative system." Though the group could not be called highly institutionalized, nevertheless "a concept arises of the group as a unique entity distinct from the constituent personalities and from all other groups." [17]

Occupational roles, we suggest, go through a similar process. A reasonable sign of institutionalization is the presence of an "indigenous normative system," which implies that between this stage and the prior stage of no role at all there is a period of time during which something is "borrowed." And what gets borrowed are clearly expectations and commitment. During this borrowed stage, persons describe what they intend to do, and what they intend role-partners to do, by referring to activities *already known*. And justification of these intentions will be based in terms of values *already held*. But in time a unique set of expectations and a commitment to their intrinsic "rightness" may emerge.[18] The indigenous stage will have been reached. Now new recruits can be brought in with less difficulty than first occupants had, though changing the role activities becomes more difficult. Thus, as was stated above, institutionalization implies the substitutability of persons but the non-substitutability of expectations.

An occupational role might be said to be institutionalized, then, when provisions exist for recruitment, training, motivation, and adaptation. But alternatively, it is institutionalized when expectations and commitment are no longer borrowed but indigenous. The investigation of institutionalization, tracing the path of its development, involves, therefore, observing how conditions are met in such a way that expectations and commitment shift (or fail to shift) from borrowed to indigenous stages.

Given variations in the surrounding conditions (which can

be assumed always to exist since persons differ "constitution-
ally," in training, in motives, and in their other roles), three
hypothetical arrangements are possible. First, the conditions
may be aligned so that persons brought together are *most
likely* to shift from the borrowed to the indigenous stage.
Second, alignment may be such that persons are brought together *randomly*. Or third, persons brought together may be
least likely to make the shift. The first arrangement yields the
highest probability that expectations will be shared and commitment to them will come about. The third arrangement
yields the highest probability that institutionalization will be
impeded.

SUMMARY

Institutionalization of the campus ministry, as was shown
in Chapter 1, has been impeded. The remaining chapters attempt to explain why. Following the analysis of the present
chapter, we shall therefore observe the conditions of recruitment, training, motivation, and adaptation, looking for ways
these are arranged so as to prevent a shift from borrowed to
indigenous expectations and commitment.

In Chapter 3 we look at the people who become campus
ministers, their attitudes and values, their various conceptions
of the position they occupy, and some of the factors that account for these variations. Chapter 4 discusses campus ministerial styles. Just as conceptions of the role differ, so also do
ways in which it is carried out. It is not surprising to find that
conceptions are reflected in activity, but there are other
highly significant influences on campus ministerial style as
well.

Chapter 5 then investigates responses to the campus ministry. How do occupants of the "counterpositions," the role-
partners, react? The strategic role-partners of a campus minis-

ter would seem to be various others on the campus and in the church; we shall observe how they respond to different campus ministers.

In Chapter 6 we return to the matter of institutionalization. Having investigated a number of elements crucial to understanding the occupation, we then assemble these elements according to our theoretical scheme in order to explain the impeded institutionalization. At that point, the entire line of analysis can be charted.

Finally, in Chapter 7, on the basis of the analysis, we discuss ways of removing or compensating for the barriers to institutionalization. The "costs" of these remedies also are discussed.

NOTES

1. It is possible to ask prior questions. For example, how did the occupation ever get conceived in the first place? And second, once conceived, how did it emerge as an identifiable activity? The reason for restricting the discussion to enacted occupational roles is obvious at this point. Accounting for persons' many transitory whims and goals clearly falls outside the scope of our interests here. Moreover, in the short run probably some people can be induced to do almost anything; our interests are in the long run, with why persons *continue* to do something.

2. Broom and Selznick identify four processes whereby associations become "institutionalized," and they correspond to the four questions above: (1) development of a distinctive social composition and social base (recruitment), (2) formalization (training), (3) infusion with value (motivation), and (4) self-maintenance and conservation (adaptation). See Leonard Broom and Philip Selznick, *Sociology* (Evanston, Ill.: Row, Peterson, 1955), pp. 237–242. See also Peter M. Blau, *Exchange and Power in Social Life* (New York: John Wiley, 1964), pp. 273–277.

3. See, for example, A. B. Shostak, "The Poverty of Welfare in America" in A. B. Shostak and W. Gomberg (eds.), *New*

Perspectives on Poverty (Englewood Cliffs, N.J.: Prentice-Hall, 1965), pp. 96 ff.

4. It should not have to be said in the context of the above discussion, but perhaps it is wiser to do so: To indicate that ignorance, poverty, or the incapacity of welfare clients to delay gratification contributes to welfare agencies' difficulty in defining their role is *not* to suggest that welfare agencies seek out middle-class clients.

5. Edward Shils supplies an example of a variant on the recruitment process, where the *absence* of appropriate qualities is not the problem but the *presence* of inappropriate qualities is. He raises the question of why politically extreme groups on the far right have had difficulty establishing a foothold in America. They have *emerged* in great number, and have always had some portion of the population as potential members, yet they typically die out after short lives. Shils suggests that, following the dynamic of most groups, they recruit as leaders those persons who best exemplify the group values, but in their case this means placing as leaders precisely those with greatest intolerance, least capacity to delegate authority, most suspicion, etc., i.e., precisely those with least leadership capacity. See his "Authoritarianism: 'Right' and 'Left'" in Richard Christie and Marie Jahoda, *Studies in the Scope and Method of "The Authoritarian Personality"* (Glencoe, Ill.: The Free Press, 1954), pp. 24–49.

6. William J. Goode, "The Librarian: From Occupation to Profession," *The Library Quarterly*, XXXI (October 1961), 311. (Italics in the original.)

7. Talcott Parsons, "Implications of the Study" in J. P. Danton, *The Climate of Book Selection* (Berkeley: University of California School of Librarianship, 1959), pp. 77–96.

8. Burton R. Clark, *Adult Education in Transition* (Berkeley and Los Angeles: University of California Press, 1958), pp. 118–120. The cited example is but one of many in Clark's analysis. Many more illustrate the scheme used above. Thus, in an effort to raise the commitment of role-partners, administrators find themselves assuming an "open-ended purpose," or "service orientation," which is not clearly defined. Consequently, the first two conditions are jeopardized: "There is no clearly delineated content (training in expecta-

tions) or clientele (recruitment of role-partners) to which the adult school can claim exclusive rights" (p. 138).

9. Waldo W. Burchard, "Role Conflicts of Military Chaplains," *American Sociological Review*, XIX (October 1954), 534.

10. Burton R. Clark, *The Open Door College* (New York: McGraw-Hill, 1960).

11. *Ibid.*, p. 2.

12. These paraphrases are drawn from *ibid.*, *passim*, but see esp. pp. 157–176.

13. Herbert Kaufman, *The Forest Ranger* (Baltimore: Johns Hopkins Press, 1960).

14. *Ibid.*, p. 207.

15. *Ibid.*, *passim*, but see esp. pp. 209–231.

16. Theodore M. Mills, *Group Transformation* (Englewood Cliffs, N.J.: Prentice-Hall, 1964), p. 74.

17. *Ibid.*, p. 76.

18. Reasons why this is the case are the subject of a growing social psychological literature. See J. W. Thibaut and H. H. Kelley, *The Social Psychology of Groups* (New York: John Wiley, 1961). Their theoretical discussion and experiments are ably applied to several institutionalizing para-psychiatric occupations in W. A. Rushing, *The Psychiatric Professions* (Chapel Hill: University of North Carolina Press, 1964).

PART II

3

THE CAMPUS

MINISTERIAL MIND

In one sense, the campus ministry has met the condition of recruitment. Fully 6 per cent of present-day Protestant seminarians plan eventually to be campus ministers.[1] Inasmuch as only 1 per cent of the current clergy are campus clergymen, church and college should have no trouble filling campus ministerial positions and doing so with considerable selectivity and/or expansion. Neither, it would appear, does the campus ministry have trouble filling counterpositions. Parish ministers, parishioners, and denominational officials—all of whom may have an interest in, and interaction with, campus ministers—are already "available" to play their parts. So it is with students, faculty, and administration on the campus. These role-partners, too, are already "recruited." By going to them, the campus minister, though he may have trouble *motivating* them to play their parts, has at least answered the question of who are the appropriate role-partners.[2]

But it is only in one sense that the recruitment condition is met. *How* it is met—with what kinds of people—is the subject of this chapter. We want, in these pages, to look at the nature of persons in the positions of chaplain and university pastor. We shall then see that, despite considerable variation within these ranks, a predominating *kind* of person is being recruited. A "campus ministerial mind" will emerge from the findings.

THE UNORTHODOXY
OF CAMPUS MINISTERS

Clergy on campus are, of course, clergymen. As obvious as that appears, it bears repeating. For, though one of the aims of this chapter is to describe the different values and attitudes among campus ministers, we should remember that the great majority (87 per cent) are ordained, and most of the remainder have had some seminary exposure. They have chosen the ministry as a vocation, have trained for it, and thus share with all ministers a great many of the characteristics distinguishing the clergy from other occupations.

Campus ministers are not representative of all ministers, however. Whether through self-selection, recruitment policy, or experiences of the campus, those who minister to higher education differ systematically from their counterparts. They are politically more liberal, have more interest in news of national and world affairs (though less in denominational news), and reveal more support for the ecumenical movement. They are more critical of their denominations, have more formal education, and are more favorable to churches' taking stronger interest in social action. In these ways, the "mind" of the campus minister differs from that of his parish colleague. Evidence is found in Table 3–1.

The evidence is convincing. The parish minister data are recent, they include ten of the same denominations used in the present study, and they permit comparisons within several age groups. The last point is especially worth emphasizing

TABLE 3–1. *The Percentage of Campus Ministers and Parish Ministers Who Agree with Various Statements*

STATEMENT	CAMPUS MINISTER (N = 997)	PARISH MINISTER (N = 3,928)*
POLITICAL ATTITUDES		
1. Strongly approve of the purposes of the United Nations	73%	57%
2. Strongly approve of the purposes of the AFL-CIO	21	11
BREADTH OF INTEREST		
3. Regularly read *Christian Century*	67	33
4. Regularly read *Christianity and Crisis*	44	6
5. Very interested in news of national and international affairs	75	62
6. Very interested in news of own denomination	35	68
7. Very or quite interested in news of other denominations	57	68
THE CHURCH AND SOCIAL ACTION		
8. Would very much like to see church-sponsored examination of major ethical issues †	66	57
9. Agree own denomination is too conservative in the field of social action	53	17
ECUMENICAL ATTITUDES		
10. Agree own denomination is not sufficiently ecumenical-minded	42	10
11. Strongly approve of the National Council of Churches	51	42
12. Strongly approve of the World Council of Churches	59	44

STATEMENT	CAMPUS MINISTER (N = 997)	PARISH MINISTER (N = 3,928)*
MISCELLANEOUS		
13. Agree own denomination does not have clearly defined policies	27	15
14. Have a Bachelor of Divinity degree	84	65
15. Have a Ph.D. degree	13	2
16. Choose, as closest to own belief regarding the Bible, "an infallible revelation of God's will" ‡	8	24

* These data were collected in 1960 by Robert E. Mitchell, then at the Bureau of Applied Social Research, Columbia University. His analysis appears in *The Professional Protestant* (forthcoming). The ten denominations he included are the same ten that include all but 29 of the 997 campus ministers of the present study. Mitchell's cooperation is gratefully acknowledged.

† The question to campus ministers read: ". . . see greater social education or action by Protestants."

‡ Other options: "inspired by God, but subject to historical criticism," and "a great history of religious experience, but not necessarily inspired by God." These two were chosen by 84 per cent and 7 per cent respectively of campus ministers, by 70 per cent and 3 per cent respectively of parish ministers.

because, though these dissimilarities might be widely acknowledged, they might also be attributed solely to the youthfulness of campus ministers, thus implying not a real but a spurious difference. Yet, in fact, denomination by denomination and age group by age group, campus and parish ministerial differences persist.[3] Campus clergy *are* systematically different from parish clergy.

How might the distinctions be summarized? Certainly one strong component underlying the items of Table 3–1 is the critical view of the organized church. Campus ministers more readily admonish their denominations for various faults. Another component is campus ministers' greater support of such agencies of change as the United Nations, the AFL-CIO, and the World Council of Churches. And a third component, over-lapping the first and second, is a greater impatience with "de-nominationalism," with the present boundaries that separate the various churches. Were one to decide on a single term to describe how campus ministers differ from parish ministers, therefore, an appropriate choice might be "unorthodox." At least in the context of their work and organizations, campus clergymen are less orthodox than their parish equivalents. They are less traditional and favor more change.[4]

CIVIL LIBERTARIANISM

Additional available information suggests that campus ministers are not merely less orthodox than other ministers. Compared with some other groups, they score as unorthodox. For example, in a poll of the American public in 1954, Stouffer discovered that 89 per cent would fire from a college faculty a person who "admits to being a Communist." Only slightly fewer (86 per cent) of the community leaders (newspaper editors, club presidents, and so forth) would do the same.[5] A year later, in 1955, Lazarsfeld and Thielens asked the same question of social-science professors in American colleges and discovered that 44 per cent held this view.[6] In 1963, when asked if an admitted Communist should be fired from a faculty post, only 16 per cent of campus ministers said yes.

It is probably true that a question like this one, asked near the height of McCarthyism and in personal interview, will evoke a more restrictive answer. Had campus ministers been questioned in a similar climate and by an interviewer rather than mail questionnaire, their answers may have been less libertarian. However, if taboos regarding domestic Communism have relaxed in the last decade, it is by no means certain that taboos regarding atheists have. The following data, therefore, lend support to the proposition that campus clergymen are relatively libertarian. The question deals with an atheist, a person who wants "to make a speech . . . against churches and religion." Table 3–2 shows the proportions of the general public, community leaders, and campus clergy who would allow such a person "to teach in a college or university." [7]

TABLE 3–2.

American public	12%
Community leaders	25%
Campus ministers (answering about a church-related college)	36%
Campus ministers (answering about a publicly supported college)	67%

Even in an area—atheism in a faculty—very important to them, campus ministers are more permissive than most Americans. But this point of view extends to other aspects of educational policy as well. Two questions dealing with proper classroom behavior, asked of social-science professors, were asked in identical or similar form of campus clergy. One inquired about the handling of "traditional values" in the lecture hall:

In teaching subjects which might require questioning of traditional values, which of these two approaches do you feel is a better educational policy for instructors to follow?
1. After proper discussion, to argue in a measured way for their own points of view.
2. To give all sides of the question impartially without revealing their own views.

Social-science professors, in 1955, chose the first answer in 38 per cent of the cases; [8] twice that proportion (77 per cent) of campus ministers did so. Granted, a campus clergyman who wants students indoctrinated with a viewpoint and who trusts that the faculty share it with him might want that viewpoint argued in the classroom. But not many situations like that can exist when (as is the case) half of all campus ministers agree that higher education is "too secular, too cavalier with students' faith," and fully three-fourths agree that higher education "does not show realistic understanding of the religious enterprise." Furthermore, the item dealt with questioning *traditional* values. Presumably, the campus minister upholds the instructor's freedom to "argue in a measured way" for scientism, humanism, materialism, or what he will, as well as for traditional points of view.

Answers to the second question on classroom policy support this interpretation. It deals with the handling of value judgments and asked:

> *Everyone agrees that many areas in a college curriculum lend themselves to value judgments. In general, in handling such matters, which emphasis do you lean to?*
>   1. Value judgments should be discussed frequently in undergraduate teaching because of the educational value of such discussion.
>   2. Instructors should answer such questions honestly when they come up but not seek out a discussion of them.
>   3. Such discussions would probably better be saved for those places and persons that are best equipped to handle them.

Among social-science faculty, 68 per cent chose the first response; among campus ministers, 73 per cent. Again the data suggest that, compared with most people, campus clergymen are quite permissive or libertarian.[9] Here are additional contributing elements of the campus ministerial mind.

THE CAMPUS MINISTERIAL MIND

These last elements, it is true, are commensurate with the earlier ones regarding political, theological, and ecclesiastical unorthodoxy. But—to repeat an earlier sentence of this chap-

ter—campus ministers are ministers. It is not surprising, therefore, to find this broader unorthodoxy expressed chiefly in
the religious sphere. When one is seeking to describe the campus ministerial mind by what distinguishes it from other
minds, here are the greatest differentiating characteristics—
the radicalism, the unorthodoxy, the impatience with tradi-
tionalism, the willingness to hear all sides—but all of these re-
dounding to the fact of the church. Unlike many radicals,
those with the campus ministerial mind do not ignore the
church; they criticize it. Unlike much unorthodoxy, the campus ministerial mind does not reject the church's heritage in
favor of a new cult; it stays within the framework of the old
even as it seeks change. And unlike libertarians in general,
those with the campus ministerial mind are chiefly desirous
that *religious* sides have hearings.

A consequence is that it is difficult for the campus ministerial mind—the unorthodoxy we are describing—to express itself without sounding critical of the church. But it is criticism
from the "inside," so to speak, not the ignoring criticism from
the outside. Perhaps not all, but many, campus ministers would
agree with the Baptist chaplain who said in an interview:

> Some of us feel that the best thing the church can do for higher
> education is to lose its students for four years and quit assum-
> ing that somehow if we lay our hands on them and bring them
> inside that we are therefore going to save them. We feel this
> approach is not working, that the best thing we can do is sim-
> ply expose students to the kinds of things a university is meant
> for—challenges and opportunities to expand their religious
> knowledge even outside the church, meaningful experience in
> worship, or in study. In other words, we should contribute to
> their religious life rather than to their church life. You would
> find within the majority of campus ministers on this campus
> the view that the church must lose itself in order to find itself.

This expression of the campus ministerial mind sounds, of
course, a good deal like the unorthodox "Fellow Citizen"

type of missionary who goes "not as a supervisor or director but as a fellow laborer. . . . It is no longer *our* attempt through *our* missionaries to carry on *our* work in distant lands." [10] But just as all missionaries do not see this as accurately descriptive of their task, neither do all campus ministers reflect equally the campus ministerial mind.

Role Conceptions of the Campus Ministry: Differentiated and Undifferentiated

The degree to which campus clergymen reflect the campus ministerial mind is a measure of their unorthodoxy (as this term is used here). Therefore, the "orthodox" persons—those least reflecting the campus ministerial mind—are orthodox in the sense that they conceive of their roles less as roles of *campus* clergymen. Instead, their task is seen to resemble more the task of the usual clergyman—the person serving the parish.[11]

The accuracy of this statement can be assessed. We can classify respondents' role conceptions—from those which most resemble the parish ministerial role to those which least resemble it. It should then turn out that respondents who conceive of their occupation in terms that differentiate it most from that of the parish minister are more unorthodox, more reflective of the campus ministerial mind. At the other extreme, respondents who conceive of their task in terms differing little from those they would use to describe the parish role should be least reflective of the campus ministerial mind.

Campus ministers were asked a number of questions applicable to a classification of role conceptions. Many of the questions dealt with the aims of the campus ministry—which of a number of listed goals are more important and which are less. Other questions inquired about respondents' motives for being clergymen on campus. These are alternative ways of asking "Why are you a campus minister?"—one asking persons what they consider desirable outcomes of a ministry in higher education, the other asking why they put themselves in the position of trying to bring about those outcomes. Together, these two types of questions tap respondents' conceptions of the role of the campus minister.

From these various questions, three were selected as indicating an *undifferentiated* conception of the campus ministry, and three were selected as indicating a *differentiated* conception. These six questions along with the proportions who agreed with each form Table 3–3.

TABLE 3–3.

Agreement Indicates Undifferentiated Role Conception	Per Cent
GOAL prepare students for participation in the church	36
GOAL help rebuild commitment to the church when it is shaken by the college experience	32
MOTIVE the church expressed the desire to have its college ministry served	48
Agreement Indicates Differentiated Role Conception	
GOAL facilitate students' religious growth even if they thereby become lost to the institutional church	56
MOTIVE felt the opportunity for a creative witness is greater in campus—than in parish—ministry	69
MOTIVE wished to avoid the routine tasks of the local parish	22

One point was assigned for each *agreement* with a differentiating item and for each *failure* to agree with an undifferentiating item. The range of scores, therefore, was 6 (very differentiated) to 0 (very undifferentiated). The number of persons in each category is shown in Table 3–4.

TABLE 3-4.

Degree of Differentiation in Role Conception	Score	N =
Much	6	44
	5	168
	4	226
Moderate	3	229
	2	172
	1	83
Little	0	21
Failed to answer one or more of the six questions		54
TOTAL		997

The Meaning of the Role-Conception Index

How are we to judge whether differentiation in conceptions of the ministerial role is adequately measured by the numbers of an index? In other words, how do we know that the index is valid? More broadly yet, how do we know what the index *means*? One answer is sometimes called face validity —the indicators of the index simply appear on face evidence to mean the same thing as the dimension underlying the distinction. Social science has relatively few indices made meaningful by face validity alone, however, so additional evidence is needed to be sure that an index is meaningful. To this evidence we now turn.

In addition to answering the three "motive" questions used in the index, campus ministers indicated the importance of six other motives they might have had for entering their special occupation. These included:

1. Felt the church was getting unfair hearing in the college community.

2. Had seen students lose interest in the church and wanted to remedy this.
3. Attracted to people who have doubts about religion.
4. Had some doubts myself and thought a campus ministry a better place to work toward their resolution.
5. Felt campus ministry offered more opportunity to think about and study theology.
6. Felt drawn by the intellectual element in this kind of work.

If we look at how persons with various role conceptions responded to these questions, several illuminating patterns are seen. First, the differentiated (23 per cent) and undifferentiated (19 per cent) [12] are alike in admitting to the first motive, though it is not very prominent for any category. The undifferentiated are somewhat more inclined to indicate the importance of the second motive (62 per cent of those with the least differentiated role conception, in contrast with 45 per cent of those with the most differentiated, say they wanted to remedy student loss to the church). But the other four motives are chosen much more often by the differentiated. "Attraction to doubters" is chosen by a majority (59 per cent) of the most differentiated but by very few (10 per cent) of the least differentiated. The most differentiated are most likely (21 per cent) to admit self-doubts; the least differentiated are least likely (0 per cent). The opportunity to think and study theology (66 per cent versus 24 per cent) and being drawn by the intellectual element (89 per cent versus 34 per cent) follow the same pattern; with each successive degree of differentiation in role conception, we observe higher rates of admitting to these motives. Together, these are the relationships we expect if a differentiated role conception means greater interest in the higher-education aspects of the ministry and less interest in "orthodox" pastoral aspects.

A second point about answers to these motive questions is this: Though the greatest difference is found with respect to the last-listed motive ("intellectual element"), even among the undifferentiated it ranks as the second most important motive.

And this leads to the third point: The differentiated in general admit to *more reasons* for being *campus* ministers.

We have some very reasonable evidence, then, for the validity of the role-conception index. Those scoring as differentiated on the index more nearly reflect the campus ministerial mind as seen by: (1) their greater admission to being drawn to that role by features unique to it, for example, intellectualism, agnosticism; (2) the fact that their motives are not so *different* from those of the undifferentiated as they are more salient or intense.

Similar points can be found in the differences in importance attached to the other "goals." "Being an available religious counselor" ranks first for all categories, but higher for the undifferentiated (100 per cent) than for the differentiated (77 per cent). All of the others, if differences exist, are more likely considered important by persons with more differentiated role conceptions, for example, "Instill in students a sustained intellectual curiosity" (68 per cent versus 19 per cent), "Develop close relationships with faculty" (48 per cent versus 24 per cent), or "Try to develop and articulate a theological basis for the campus ministry" (32 per cent versus 14 per cent).

There were many more questions which help to put flesh on the bones of a quantitative index. Several of these asked for agreement or disagreement with certain general criticisms of higher education. Another asked which of three labels a respondent would most likely use to describe his present ministry.[13] Still another is the question—already seen—asking whether an atheist should be allowed to remain on the faculty of a church-related school and on the faculty of a publicly supported school. And finally is the matter of whose opinions are considered more important in evaluating a campus ministry.[14] The relationships between these questions and the role-conception index can be summarized in this manner:

1. Persons with undifferentiated role conceptions of the campus ministry are more likely to judge higher education as too secular for students' faith, whereas those with differentiated role conceptions are more critical of the "applied" and "frilly" features they see in universities. Campus ministers of any role conception, however, are most critical of higher education for its apparent unrealistic understanding of religion.

2. The undifferentiated are far more likely to see themselves as "pastors"; the differentiated see themselves more as "religious voices" in the academy or as "teaching ministers."

3. The differentiated are more likely to allow atheism to be represented on college faculties, thus suggesting that, as campus ministers differ in "libertarianism" from the general public, so do differentiated campus clergy differ from undifferentiated.

4. In choosing important "evaluators" of their work, the undifferentiated select more from within the denomination (parish ministers and officials); the differentiated select more from higher education (administration, faculty, seminary teachers) and their colleagues.

Again the evidence supports the imputed meaning of the index: Differentiated role conceptions more nearly reflect the campus ministerial mind. Any remaining doubt should disappear, moreover, when it is pointed out that *every item used at the beginning of this chapter to distinguish the campus ministerial mind*—from that of parish ministers, of the general public, of community leaders, and of social scientists—*also distinguishes between the differentiated and undifferentiated in role conception.* The former, one might say, are more "campus ministerial" than the latter.[15]

Consider the following quotations from personal interviews

with two university pastors, one a Methodist at a large state university, the other a Baptist at a small state school.

The Methodist: Some conceive of the campus ministry in terms of a building, and the task is to get students to come and be active. Effectiveness, then, is judged in terms of where *we* are rather than in terms of where things are going on. They try to get students out of the environment of the university and increase their association with the church, rather than feel their way in to discover what the university is, what students are believing and what problems they are living with. This latter is an image of a mission that is hard for some to think of. Instead of gathering students away from this "devastating" university situation that corrupts their morals and robs their faith, it seems to me that the exciting part of the work is right at the other axis, where the normal flow of university life is.

The Baptist: I think my major task is to break down students' ignorance of the church, to make them grow in this area as they are growing in other academic fields. This means tearing down a lot of superstitions that exist within our Protestant denominations. Some of the churches students come from have not been very inspiring; most of them have a second or third grade knowledge of their faith. We have to challenge them with what the church ought to be, and they've got a lot of growing to do. It would not bother me if the student rejects the church or tends to become an atheist. If he is beginning to question, this is fine; from there we can begin to build.

Campus ministers with differentiated conceptions of their role would agree with these two statements; those with undifferentiated conceptions would agree only in part.

The Sources of Different Role Conceptions

Chaplains and university pastors differ considerably in role conception. More than half (57 per cent) of the chaplains have differentiated role conceptions (that is, scores of 6, 5, 4) in contrast with 43 per cent of university pastors. But whether chaplains or university pastors, campus ministers from denominations with strong liturgical tradition (Lutheran, Episcopal) or with more conservative theology (Southern Baptist, Presbyterian, U.S.) are less likely to be differentiated in their orientation to the campus ministry. (See Table 3–5.)

TABLE 3–5.

DENOMINATION	PER CENT DIFFERENTIATED (SCORES OF 6, 5, 4)	NO. OF CASES ON WHICH PERCENTAGE IS BASED
Disciples	69	32
United Church of Christ	61	69
Presbyterian, U.S.A.	57	103
Methodist	56	262
American Baptist	54	63
Lutheran (National Lutheran Council)	46	76
Episcopal	31	120
Southern Baptist	31	121
Presbyterian, U.S.	29	41
Miscellaneous *	29	28
Missouri Synod Lutheran	14	28

* Evangelical and United Brethren, Reformed Church, Unitarian, and others. See Appendix for description of how persons were selected.

But denomination and position as chaplain or university pastor by no means wholly determine role conception. Amount of formal education is another factor which cuts across denominational lines. The more education, the more differentiated is the orientation.[16] And, of specific interest to this discussion, another influence on role conception is the factor of specialized preparation for the campus ministry. By now, a number of seminaries offer courses designed to prepare campus ministers, several denominations and a private foundation offer "internships" enabling trainees to spend a year under the supervision of experienced campus clergy, and "workshops" or other short-term programs exist as devices to train campus ministers. The proportion in the study who have had each type of training is shown in Table 3–6.

TABLE 3–6.

Training	
Internship *	5%
Seminary course(s)	22
Workshop	4
Training indicated but unspecified	1
No special training	68
	100%

* Persons who have been interns *and* had seminary courses are classed as having had an "internship." Those with courses *and* workshop are classed as having had "seminary course(s)."

In addition to these programs, however, an important source of training for the campus ministry is reading material, some bearing directly on religion in higher education, some more indirectly concerned, such as character education or the governing of higher education. The reading lists in seminary courses for campus ministers will typically contain materials of this sort, but we wanted to know how familiar campus ministers are in general with literature bearing on their work. They were asked, therefore, whether they had read certain books, the first three dealing with "religion" in education, the second three dealing with the values and attitudes of college students. These books, and the proportions who had read them, are listed in Table 3–7. The books on "religion" were

TABLE 3–7.

	READ BY
Peter Berger, *The Noise of Solemn Assemblies*	68%
Alexander Miller, *Faith and Learning*	58
Walter Moberly, *The Crisis in the University*	55
Allan Barton, *Studying the Effects of College Education*	4
Rose Goldsen, *et al.*, *What College Students Think*	23
Philip Jacob, *Changing Values in College*	53

more frequently read, as was anticipated, than "secular" books on college students' values. In constructing an index of special preparation, we therefore assigned a campus minister one point for each of these characteristics: (1) having read *two* or more of the first three books listed; (2) having read *one* or more of the second three books listed; (3) having had *any* type of specialized training. The highest score became 3 on this index, and the lowest 0. (See Table 3–8.)

TABLE 3–8.

SCORE		N =
3	Very high special preparation	181
2	High special preparation	351
1	Low special preparation	276
0	Very low special preparation	176
	Did not answer one or more questions	13
	TOTAL	997

One effect of specialized preparation for the campus ministerial role is greater differentiation in conceiving that role. Over half (55 per cent) of the persons with very high special preparation have differentiated role conceptions in contrast with fewer than a third (32 per cent) of those with very low special preparation. The first proportion increases to two-thirds among possessors of degrees beyond the B.D. who are from "liberal" or "non-liturgical" denominations, and the second proportion drops to one-fifth among those from other denominations possessing no more than a B.D. or Master's degree. The impact of special preparation is maintained in all of these categories. It is quite clear, in other words, that, irrespective of their denomination, campus ministers' education, and especially a certain kind of "education" conveyed through specialized training and literature, tends to produce differentiated conceptions of the campus clergyman's role. Insofar as churches urge their campus clergy to take more formal education, and inasmuch as internships, seminary courses, and workshops are directly and indirectly supported by churches, then to this extent churches encourage differentiation of the sort discussed in this chapter.

Denominational officials, for the most part, would not blanch at this conclusion. They are aware of the specialized nature of the campus ministry and aware, therefore, of the necessity for unusual approaches to it.

THE FUNCTION OF ROLE CONCEPTIONS

Differentiation of the role of campus minister is clearly occurring. Having begun six decades ago with conceptions resembling those of the parish ministry, the campus ministry can claim now to be moving in the direction of a distinctive set of expectations. As the amount and specialized nature of the campus clergymen's education increase, such differentiation can be expected to continue. It already appears with greater frequency among younger campus ministers, who are the more likely recipients of more and special education.

As significant as its shape or content, however, is the fact that it *is* a role conception; the campus ministry may be evolving a unifying philosophy of its task.

In 1920, a pioneer campus minister circulated a card entitled "What Is the Work of the University Pastor?" His answer:

> To become acquainted with the students; . . . to help them find rooms and employment; to inform them about the location and services of the churches; to induce them to enroll in Bible and mission classes; to introduce them to each other and to the members of the churches; . . . to provide for their social life; . . . to teach classes in Bible and mission studies; to establish close personal relations with students; . . . to help them in their intellectual difficulties, religious doubts, and trying Christian experiences; to minister to them in sickness; to stimulate them to their best endeavor in their university work; to advise them, when undecided, relative to vocations; to bring them the claims of Christ in their lives; to keep them in intelligent touch with the work . . . of the denomination; to cultivate in them a spirit of service; . . . to discover in them capacity for the work of the ministry . . . and find recruits for these vocations; to co-operate with other Christian agencies and forces in creating a better religious environment in the university.[17]

However, the question "What is the work of a campus minister?" can no longer be answered by a list. All campus ministers even today would agree with all these objectives, with perhaps a little amendment. But who can pursue them all—successfully and equally well and simultaneously? Obviously decisions have to be made to decrease attention in one place in order to increase it in another. Such decisions, when they occur, are made in terms of values; a role conception is a ranking of values, an establishment of priorities, and thus a way of making decisions according to some coherent plan. This is the function of role conceptions.

Differences in role conceptions do not *necessarily* mean

differences in activity; the former indicate what ought to be done, the latter what actually is done. In the next chapter, however, we shall see that persons differing in role conceptions do indeed behave in markedly different ways.

NOTES

1. As reported in a study of 17,565 seminary students by K. R. Bridston and D. W. Culver in *Seminary Quarterly*, V (Spring 1964), 2.
2. Cuninggim, *The College Seeks Religion*, argues that university personnel are not only available to play their parts but also willing and anxious to do so. In Chapter 5 we have more to say about this.
3. Using three age groups in ten denominations, each of the questions in Table 3–1 can be assessed 30 times. With 16 questions, 480 comparisons of parish and campus ministers are possible. Of these, 89 per cent reveal the difference contained in Table 3–1, though of the 11 per cent which do not, a quarter involve cells containing fewer than 10 cases.
4. The consequences of this difference for Protestant organizations are traced in P. E. Hammond and R. E. Mitchell, "Segmentation of Radicalism: The Case of the Protestant Campus Minister," *American Journal of Sociology*, LXXI (1965), 133–143. Of course, "orthodoxy" has many meanings in many different contexts. One of the justifications for the length of this section is to make clear what the term means here.
5. S. A. Stouffer, *Communism, Conformity and Civil Liberties* (New York: Doubleday, 1955), pp. 40–43.
6. Paul F. Lazarsfeld and W. Thielens, *The Academic Mind* (Glencoe, Ill.: The Free Press, 1958), pp. 391–392.
7. The full wording and answers are found in Stouffer, *op. cit.*, pp. 32–33. The question to campus ministers was slightly different: "Suppose now another man—one who advocates atheism and is opposed to all religious institutions as commonly understood—is teaching in a college. If it were a church-related college, do you think he ought to be released from his position?" Then: "If the college were publicly supported, should he be let go?"

8. Lazarsfeld and Thielens, *op. cit.*, p. 135, discuss this and the next question.

9. Indeed, in some schools the campus ministers may be in a position to be more protective of academic freedom than the faculty. For example, the [Little Rock] *Arkansas Gazette* reported on November 28, 1964, a faculty "resolution assailing the University [of Arkansas] administration for screening speakers." The resolution backed the university pastor of the Wesley Foundation, "who let a Communist official use the Wesley Foundation facilities to speak when the University denied the official the use of a building."

10. See above, p. 10 and p. 8. Another sketch suitably descriptive of the campus ministerial mind, this one of a type of seminary student and therefore with an accented intellectual component, is found in H. R. Niebuhr, D. Williams, and J. Gustafson, *The Advancement of Theological Education* (New York: Harper, 1957), pp. 156–158.

11. Cantelon, *A Protestant Approach to the Campus Ministry*, pp. 14–15.

12. These percentages are for the extreme categories of "most" and "least" differentiation. Here, as with successive instances, the middle categories on the index of differentiation have correspondingly "middle" percentages.

13. The three: "a pastor to counsel people in the college community in matters of faith and vocation," "a teaching minister, to advance religious knowledge in the educational process," or "a religious voice in the academic community, to reveal added dimensions in secular education."

14. The question reads: "In his work, everyone knows persons whose evaluation he regards more than others. Here are several groups who may have opinion of your ministry. Please indicate the three whose opinion you consider the more important: parish clergy in your denomination; officials in your denomination; college administration; faculty; seminary teacher; other campus ministers."

15. It is instructive to note, however, that generally speaking even the least differentiated of campus ministers resemble "average," not "conservative," parish ministers; they resemble liberal, not conservative, community leaders, etc. For all of its diversity, then, the campus ministry has an occupational "culture."

16. Thus, 30 per cent of those with only a Bachelor's or Master's (chiefly M.Ed.) degree have differentiated role conceptions, 46 per cent of those with B.D., 50 per cent of those with B.D. plus Master's degree, and 59 per cent of those with a doctorate degree.

17. Quoted in Shedd, *The Church Follows Its Student*, p. 66.

4

STYLES OF THE
CAMPUS MINISTRY

From some standpoint, what campus ministers *do* is more significant than what they think they *ought* to do. Having seen in the previous chapter something of the range and patterns of campus ministerial values, we turn in this section to a discussion of how campus clergy in fact spend their time. Our purpose is: (1) to chart systematic differences in the activities of campus ministers—we shall call these "styles"—and (2) to determine some of the forces, individual and contextual, that produce different styles.[1]

THE ACTIVITIES OF
CAMPUS MINISTERS

A British theologian, following his observation of American campuses after World War II, wrote:

America has more full-time students' chaplains . . . than any other country in the world. Yet while a number of these gentlemen show, to the astonished admiration of European visitors, a virtuosity in devising spontaneous entertainments equal to that of the great Danny Kaye himself, their intellectual responsibilities appear to sit very lightly upon their shoulders. With a few shining exceptions their purpose in the university appears to be to run a bigger and better young people's group than in the church back home.[2]

What may have been a fair assessment in 1949 certainly would not be today, however. "Social and recreational concerns began to be replaced, or at least supplemented and enriched, by study retreats and conferences," writes one observer.[3] Another comments on "a silent revolution . . . in progress for more than a decade now. . . . Particularly since the early fifties, campus ministry has undergone extensive change."[4]

Some of this "extensive change," together with evidence that older patterns of activity are still popular, can be seen in Table 4–1, which shows the answers to the question: "Here

TABLE 4–1. *The Frequency (in Percentages *) of Sixteen Activities*

	QUITE FREQUENTLY	OCCASIONALLY	RARELY OR NEVER
1. Engaged in informal theological discussions with students	71%	26%	1%
2. Given personal counseling to students or faculty	68	29	1
3. Helped students organize religious programs	60	32	6
4. Led formal study groups on religious topics	48	40	10
5. Entertained students in your home	47	45	6
6. Conducted worship service for the campus	32	24	42

	QUITE FREQUENTLY	OCCASIONALLY	RARELY OR NEVER
7. Been active in own denomination's regional or national meetings on matters other than the campus ministry	20	45	33
8. Had sessions for students becoming baptized, confirmed, church members, and so forth	16	23	59
9. Been liaison for local church to get faculty or other adults into the life of the church	15	37	46
10. Engaged in theological discussions with faculty	14	60	24
11. Helped students organize social events	13	43	42
12. Helped students organize some social action effort	10	50	38
13. Taken stands you knew your denomination would disapprove of	6	44	48
14. Taken stands you knew the college administration would disapprove of	5	50	43
15. Guest-lectured for some faculty member	1	23	74
16. Had meetings for college alumni to discuss religious and social issues	1	8	89

* Percentages do not total 100 because 2 per cent in each case failed to answer.

are a number of things campus ministers might do. In the past year how frequently have you done each of them: quite frequently, occasionally, rarely or never?" The first two activities—informal theological discussions with students and personal counseling—are practically universal. Almost everyone does these things at least occasionally. Correlatively, the last two on the list—guest-lecturing for faculty and ministering to college alumni—are very rare activities. In between are the dozen activities that many engage in but many do not. Campus ministerial styles, if they are to be identified, will be found within these twelve.[5]

It is possible, by cross-tabulating each item of activity with every other item, to discover whether persons engaging in one activity are more likely to engage in certain others as well. Thus, if those who engage in A are more likely to engage in B and C than are those who do not engage in A, we may refer to a "cluster" of activities. Especially if A, B, and C have some commonality, so that their clustering suggests a particular underlying dimension, it is appropriate to think of persons as located at various points along this underlying dimension. Indeed, it is in just this way that many concepts and labels have entered our language and thought. Thus, "pessimism" in people or "realism" in art, as dimensions or properties, can be applied to all people or all paintings. Some persons exhibit so few indications of pessimism (seldom glum, infrequently predict dire events) as to be regarded rather as optimistic, just as some paintings are so cameralike in color, size, form, and so forth, as to be regarded as very realistic. The assignment of some degree of pessimism-optimism or of realism-abstractness, then, is based on the observation that "clusterings" of attributes occur, and units differentially share in them.[6] Were this not so, much of the meaning of such classificatory concepts as pessimism or realism would be lost.

So it is with the activities of campus ministers. Cross-tabulation of the various items reveals two clusters, one consisting of Numbers 4, 10, and 12 ("formal study groups on religious topics"; "theological discussions with faculty"; "social action"), the other of Numbers 3, 9, and 11 ("organize religious programs"; "liaison for local church"; "organize social events"). The contents of the clusters, furthermore, suggest an underlying dimension, each set of items representing one "end" of that dimension. The three items in the first cluster are marks of the "silent revolution" or "extensive change" mentioned above, just as the three items in the second cluster mark the older "social and recreational concerns," the "holding the faithful or recovering the fallen." [7] The first set represents innovation, the second set the pastoral tradition with which the campus ministry began. Instead of religious programs with a series of speakers, there is formal study of religion. Instead of social events, there is social action or service. Instead of drawing faculty into the life of the church, there is engagement with faculty in theological discussion. The changing philosophy of the campus ministry (seen above in Chapter 1), and the changing conceptions of the campus ministerial role (Chapter 3), here find their analogue in the various styles of conducting a campus ministry. The "colonial administrator" versus "fellow citizen" and the "undifferentiated" versus "differentiated" have a parallel in the area of activities—"pastoral" versus "innovative."

STYLES OF THE CAMPUS MINISTRY

Each of the six items forming the two clusters are engaged in frequently, occasionally, or rarely or never by all campus ministers. By assigning two, one, or no points to these categories, then adding the number of points each person receives on three innovative activities and on three traditional activities, we arrive at two scores for every individual. First is a score for the frequency with which he engages in innovative activities (6 if he does all three frequently; 0 if he does all three rarely or never), and second is a score for the frequency with which he engages in pastoral activities. Scores of six on both scales indicate frequent engagement in all of these activities, just as scores of zero on both scales indicate rare engagement in any of them.[8] Next, by cross-tabulating the two scores we arrive at a single classification device, ranging from Most Innovative (persons scoring 5 or 6 on the innovative items but 0–2 on the pastoral items) to Most Pastoral (persons scoring 5 or 6 on the pastoral items but 0–2 on the innovative items). In the middle are persons whose two scores are an equal mixture between innovative and pastoral. (See Table 4–2.)

TABLE 4–2.

	N =
Most innovative	34
Quite innovative	130
Somewhat innovative	207
Mixed	277
Somewhat pastoral	164
Quite pastoral	117
Most pastoral	35
Failed to answer one or more questions	33
TOTAL	997

This index of style has its internal logic, as we have seen, but in addition several key relationships which substantiate the meaning of the index can be shown. For example, one of the innovations in campus religious work has been the idea that campus clergy stand in a position to criticize both the church and higher education. Drawing upon the resources and stimulation from either sphere, campus ministers are especially able to criticize, judge, and challenge both spheres. At least, this would seem to be the notion that lies behind such popular statements as "The campus minister should be an enabler," "He should lead from the middle," "He should help the church be the church and the university be the university." Unless one has some notion of campus clergy as critics, these statements are meaningless at best, ludicrous at worst. If the index of style really distinguishes between innovative and pastoral ministries, then this distinction ought to be reflected in the "critical" behavior of those with different scores on the index. And indeed it is. Among the items of Table 4–1 are two questions about taking stands "known to be disapproved" by denomination and college administration (Numbers 13 and 14). Neither of these is reported as a very frequent activity, but the first is reported by 53 per cent of the Most Innovative as at least an occasional activity, and the second kind of stand is reported by 82 per cent. These rates drop with each successive category down to the Most Pastoral, of whom only 34 per cent report taking denominationally disapproved stands and a mere 20 per cent report occasionally taking the other. The implication is strong, therefore, that with innovation goes the tendency to be critical or challenging.

With other questions comes another insight into pastoral and innovative styles. Respondents were asked how much personal satisfaction they derived from contacts with students active in their programs and with students who were not active. They were also asked about personal satisfaction from contacts with faculty who are active in church and those who are not. With innovative style comes a modest decline in satisfaction from "active" students, a greater decline in satisfaction from "active" faculty, and a remarkable *increase* in satisfaction derived from nonactive students and faculty. This relationship is so pronounced, in fact, that among Most or Quite Innovative campus ministers, nonactive students provide as much satisfaction as active students, and nonactive faculty supply considerably more than active faculty.

But what is the appearance of an innovative campus ministry? The traditional, pastoral style is fairly well understood because it has been around for so long. According to one observer, it

> conjures up a series of images similar to the following: a Sunday-night supper with many wholesome teenagers devouring hot dogs, casseroles, and ice cream; a "student worker," young, handsome, likable, and popular, who is milling about meeting newcomers and sharing the good time with the regulars; a songfest . . . around a piano singing "Jacob's Ladder" and "Lord, I Want to Be a Christian"; a hay ride; a weekend retreat; and a remodeled nineteenth-century house on College Avenue which serves as a "denominational fellowship center" equipped with a hi-fi set, Ping-pong tables, a small shelf of books, and the inevitable soft drink dispenser.[9]

The innovative ministry, though inevitably sharing some of the same characteristics with the pastoral, is somewhat harder to describe. On some campuses, it takes the form of "faith and life communities," where the campus clergyman gathers around him a small number of students who live, worship, study, and play together in a single dwelling for a semester or a year—and may do so under disciplinary vows reminiscent of some monasteries. On other campuses, elaborate programs of social service—remedial work with educationally deprived children, counseling of delinquents, supervision of recreation for impoverished youth—are conducted under the aegis of the religious ministry, and the campus clergyman administers these programs. On still other campuses, the experimental theater, the lecture series with off-campus spokesmen, or the special seminars for commuter students or graduate students' wives, are conducted by campus ministers.[10]

In each of these cases, the activity of the campus ministry deviates from the pastoral style. It tends to involve less use of a "center"; the campus minister engages his clients in their setting, not his. It builds on the university curriculum, enlisting the cooperation of departments or professional schools in jointly sponsored lectures, for example, rather than offering alternative lectures. It seeks to involve students and faculty in off-campus issues. It may enlist proportionately fewer clients but may ask more of them, for example, a study group with a series of books rather than Sunday-night suppers followed by speakers. Though no campus ministry will include only these kinds of elements ("everyone," remember, at least occasionally counsels and discusses theology informally with students), the more innovative will include at least some of them.

SOURCES OF INNOVATIVE STYLE

In Chapter 1, it was seen that chaplains have less contact with, and less formal responsibility to, their denominations than do university pastors. Since innovative campus ministries involve less "holding the faithful and recovering the fallen," that is, less focus on students of one's own denomination and more on the campus as a whole, we might expect chaplains to be more innovative. This is not the case, however; they are somewhat less likely to score in one of the three innovative categories on the index of style (35 per cent versus 40 per cent). One explanation lies no doubt in the greater circumscription of the chaplaincy. Most chaplains are employed to conduct worship in the college chapel and teach part time in religion or philosophy departments. Their opportunity to engage in new types of ministry, and thus be classified as innovative, is therefore reduced.

But if the circumscription of campus ministerial position influences style, so also does the role conception of its occupant. Quite naturally, what people feel they ought to do is reflected in what they in fact do. The more differentiated a campus clergyman's conception of his role, the more likely is he to carry out that role in innovative fashion. Thus, 45 per cent of those with differentiated role conceptions, 37 per cent classed as moderate, and 20 per cent classed as undifferentiated are innovative. These differences, moreover, are even greater for university pastors (and therefore less for chaplains), which lends support to the statement just above that the less circumscribed position allows greater opportunity for role conception to influence style of activity.

Still another factor influencing style is the degree of special preparation, an attribute observed in Chapter 3 to have some impact on role conception. We can note, however, that in addition to its influence on style as *mediated through* role conception, the factor of special preparation exerts an *independent* force as well. The more specialized training for the campus ministry a man has had, the more likely he is to engage in innovative activity, irrespective of the degree of differentiation he demonstrates on the role-conception index. But even this statement can be refined: Specialized preparation exerts more influence on those with less-differentiated role conceptions or, correlatively, a differentiated role conception has more impact on those with low special preparation than on those with high special preparation. It is as though *either* of these characteristics increases the likelihood of innovation in style, but *both together* have little more impact than either does separately. True, the very low in preparation whose role conception is undifferentiated are *least* likely to be innovative (16 per cent); and the highly prepared who also have a differentiated conception of their role are *most* likely to be innovative (57 per cent). But in terms of the probability of any change in style, the two factors are almost interchangeable.[11] Two paths are suggested, therefore: the path of differentiated values and the path of specialized training. Either path leads to innovation in style of activity.

SUMMARY

In Chapter 3, we observed that experience in specialized courses, internships, or workshops, and exposure to specialized literature on religion in higher education were associated with a tendency toward conceiving a differentiated role of the campus minister. In that discussion, specialized preparation was treated as if it *produces* differentiation, although it might be the case that persons with different role conceptions *seek out* different preparatory experiences. In the present chapter, we may conclude that the proper causal order of those two variables ceases to be an important question since each is independently related to style. Instead, the causal order of both with style becomes the crucial question. Are innovative campus ministries *products* of preparation and differentiated role conceptions or do innovative campus ministers *seek out* their specialized preparation and *create* distinctive role conceptions to rationalize their activity? The response, of course, without measures from more than one point in time, has to be that it is impossible to know for sure. The probable causal order must be assessed on inferential grounds.

Since the discussion above has been presented *as if* style is produced by these other factors, it is important to indicate the inferential basis for our assumption. The chief inference is that of time order; certainly one's formal education (seminary courses, internships) precedes his full-time involvement as a campus minister. Insofar as formal education and style are related, then, the latter can more reasonably be entertained as a result of the former (though it may result from other factors as well). Informal education continues, however, as literature is read and experiences which may mold role conceptions continue. How do we know that a campus minister of traditional, pastoral style, say, does not read only material and engage in only those experiences which maintain his belief that the pastoral style is proper? How do we know, in other words, but what persons simply create their own "worlds" of experience according to their patterns of behavior, rather than develop patterns of behavior to accord with their worlds of experience?

One answer is this: If we find situations which cannot be influenced *by* persons but which instead may be influential *on* them, then the basis for assessing direction of influence (or causation) is quite strong. We can only infer, then, that role conceptions and different levels of specialized preparation influence style, rather than the reverse. And we so infer because it is less reasonable to view churches, seminaries, publication of books, and discussions of campus ministerial aims as subject to change by individual campus clergymen than it is to view individuals as subject to change by the nature and degree of their exposure to these other factors. But if we are left with having to infer the direction of influence of preparation and role conception on style, we are on considerably firmer ground in tracing the impact of another factor—the context in which styles of activity are carried out —and the findings here lend support to the influence above.

Campuses as Contexts for Styles of Activity

All but a very few campus clergymen serve single campuses. Even the handful who operate in a multicampus situation have specifiable locations in which their clients or potential clients can be found. Contexts for the campus ministry, in other words, are given; the ministry focuses on those contexts and the people in them. Yet, the contexts vary enormously, as much as higher education itself. A chaplain may minister to a small, unaccredited junior college or to an elite, private university. A university pastor may be in a rural teachers' college, a huge land-grant state university, or a nebulous commuter college in the middle of city commercial traffic. That the context for his work should influence a campus minister's style seems hardly doubtful, but just what the relationship may be is the question to which we now turn.

Certainly one notable and meaningful way in which academic communities differ is in their "cosmopolitanism," quite literally, the extent to which they are composed of "citizens of the world." Schools whose student bodies and faculties are drawn from all over are more cosmopolitan than those which draw only from local populations. Curricula with wide ranges of offerings are more cosmopolitan than those containing few courses. Campuses providing access to variegated off-campus experiences are more cosmopolitan than isolated campuses. The presence of foreign students, graduate students, and extension students, the enrollment or employment of Catholic, Protestant, Jew, and non-believer, the possibility of playing or watching lacrosse and water polo as well as football and basketball, of attending debates as well as lectures, of hearing Cage and Corelli as well as Beethoven and Brahms—all these and more indicate cosmopolitan, in contrast with local, campuses.

Measurement of cosmopolitanism is more difficult than illustrating it, however. Is the Washington Square campus of New York University with its ready access to subways and symphonies, bookstores and "beat" cafés, really more cosmopolitan than a Midwestern agricultural college that offers animal husbandry and a yearly rodeo as well as courses in existential philosophy? The question is raised not to prove the impossibility of measuring the concept—people, after all, use the term with some precision and mutual understanding—but to indicate that however it is measured, cosmopolitanism is situational—that is, relative to time and place—at least implicitly.

In the case of American colleges and universities generally, the situation by which cosmopolitanism is assessed is fairly clear. Higher education in America was once restricted to small, church-related schools whose students were almost all Protestant. Over the years, the size of schools has grown; publicly controlled and many private, independent colleges have come into being; and Protestantism can no longer be automatically assumed in student bodies. Cosmopolitanism on American campuses, therefore, though a *result* of many forces and potentially different for different persons, is reasonably well *indicated* by increasing size, increasing religious heterogeneity in the student body, and control by independent or public boards rather than by churches.[12] Campus ministers are found in situations representing all combinations of these factors and thus in contexts differing widely in cosmopolitanism.[13]

According to information supplied by respondents, the schools to which they minister were assigned points on the basis of: (1) three sizes of student body (under 2,500; 2,500–8,999; 9,000 or more), (2) three categories by proportion of students from Protestant background (90 per cent or more; 50 per cent–89 per cent; 49 per cent or less), and (3) type of support (church-related; public; private non-denominational). The most cosmopolitan campus is thus a private independent school with a student body of 9,000 or more, fewer than half of which are Protestant in background.[14] The least cosmopolitan (most "local") is a church-related school of fewer than 2,500 students of whom 90 per cent or more are Protestant in background. Differences in cosmopolitanism make for radically different contexts in which to be a campus minister, as will now be shown.

LOCAL AND COSMOPOLITANISM
CONTEXTS

Respondents were asked to characterize students at their school in several ways, chiefly by how much they engage in various student endeavors. As their answers make clear, "local" and "cosmopolitan" campuses are quite different things. At least, campus ministers see them in markedly different ways. At the "local" extreme there is more extracurricular activity and interest in religious questions; at the "cosmopolitan" extreme, more attention to academic and political affairs and competition for grades. And, of most immediate importance, with cosmopolitanism comes a radical decrease in student participation in campus religious organizations.

Given decidedly different contexts in which to work, campus clergymen not surprisingly conduct quite different ministries. Placed in diverse environments, they respond with diverse kinds of activity; cosmopolitanism produces innovative style. We have already observed how, among chaplains and university pastors alike, those with more specialized preparation and differentiated role conceptions are more likely to be innovative in style. Now it can be seen that school cosmopolitanism has an additional effect.

The effect of role conception and specialized preparation is maintained in Table 4–3, as seen in the decreasing rates of innovation as one reads down the columns. But, in addition, the cosmopolitanism of the campus renders style more innovative, and it does so *irrespective* of the individual's role conception and preparation (seen by reading across the rows). The relationships hold true for both chaplains and university pastors.

There is another important observation to be made indirectly from Table 4–3: By noting the numbers of cases on which percentages are based, one can see that persons with

TABLE 4–3. *Effect of Cosmopolitanism on the Style of Campus Ministers Differing in Role Conception and Special Preparation*

PER CENT INNOVATIVE WHEN DEGREE OF DIFFERENTIATION AND AMOUNT OF SPECIAL PREPARATION (COMBINED *) IS	VERY OR QUITE LOCAL	SOMEWHAT LOCAL OR SOMEWHAT COSMOPOLITAN	VERY OR QUITE COSMOPOLITAN
Very high	31 (29)	54 (61)	55 (86)
High	27 (37)	42 (52)	54 (90)
Medium	32 (47)	45 (74)	50 (70)
Low	37 (41)	34 (59)	31 (68)
Very low	6 (67)	24 (67)	21 (67)

* This index is the combination of special preparation (3 categories: High or Very High; Low; Very Low) and role conception (3 categories: Much differentiation; Some; Moderate or Little). Very High on this index = High or Very High Preparation plus Much Differentiation; High on this index = High or Very High Preparation plus Some Differentiation *or* Low Preparation plus Much Differentiation, and so forth. The figures in parentheses are the number of cases on which percentages are based.

differentiated role conceptions and higher preparation are more often found in cosmopolitan schools. Though this is true of chaplains as well as university pastors, the great majority of chaplains are nevertheless found on local campuses, that is, church-related schools with fewer students but proportionately more Protestants. Although this latter fact is hardly surprising, it does offer another explanation for our earlier finding that chaplains are less innovative in style. Because more of them are in local schools, the pressures are less on them to deviate from the traditional, pastoral campus ministerial style. The data indicate, however, that when chaplains are placed in more cosmopolitan settings, their likelihood of innovating is equal to, if not in excess of, that of university pastors.

SUMMARY

Midway in this chapter the question of establishing causal order was raised. At that time it was said, "If we find situations which cannot be influenced *by* persons but which instead may be influential *on* them, then the basis for assessing direction of influence (or causation) is quite strong." [15] The cosmopolitanism-style relationship is such a situation. Campus ministers can hardly be said to influence a school's cosmopolitanism (at least its size, control, and proportion of student body which is Protestant). At most, persons who are predisposed to innovation could seek out cosmopolitanism. On the other hand, the extent to which a school deviates from the historical model of the small Protestant college can very reasonably be said to cause campus clergymen to respond with programs of activity different from the pastoral one. The historical development of higher education produces change in the style of the campus ministry.

Since this is the case, we have a somewhat firmer basis for inferring the causal order of the special preparation-style and role conception-style relationships. For these factors, too, represent historical development in the campus ministry—from no *specialized* preparation to more, and from undifferentiated to differentiated aims. Indeed, without too much exaggeration, the implied causal sequence can be stated thus: (1) As the units of higher education change from small, homogeneous Protestant organizations to huge, cosmopolitan structures with no formal relationship to the church, the aims of the church in its ministry to academic communities also change. (2) To conduct its ministry, the church develops special literature, courses, and other training devices in order that its representatives will be better equipped to confront changing higher education. (3) One result is modification in how the campus ministerial role is conceived, which in turn (4) modifies the actual behavior of campus ministers. (5) Finally, however, changing higher education exerts pressure directly on campus ministers' behavior, and does so irrespective of persons' exposure to specialized preparation and modified role conceptions.

Once again the foreign-missions analogy is instructive. As the world changes, so also do foreign missionaries change, in part because of different training, in part because of modifications in their aims, and in part because of the exigencies of the missionary situation. So it is with the campus ministry. Among campus ministers serving "very local" campuses, those with little or no special preparation and with an undifferentiated role conception very likely will be pastoral in style (89 per cent). Conversely, those with a differentiated role conception and special preparation who serve "very cosmopolitan" campuses very likely will be innovative in style (67 per cent). The occupation changes according to the forces—individual and collective—that impinge on it. Why this should be and with what consequences are the topics of the next chapter.

NOTES

1. Others have reported how campus ministers distribute their time. See Clarence Shedd, *The Church Follows Its Students*, p. 262; Seymour Smith, *The American College Chaplaincy*, pp. 75, 109; J. C. Windsor and T. W. Wright, "The American Higher Educational Chaplain," *Chapel and College* (Spring 1963), pp. 19–35.
2. Daniel Jenkins, "The Crisis in the University," *Christianity and Crisis*, IX (1949), 166.
3. Myron M. Teske in George L. Earnshaw (ed.), *The Campus Ministry* (Valley Forge: The Judson Press, 1964), p. 106.

4. LeRoy S. Loats in Earnshaw, *op. cit.*, p. 302. See also the essay by Broholm, pp. 257–276.

5. Respondents could answer, of course, only about activities supplied them in the list. Writing, for example, or lecturing around the country, or involvement in foreign-student exchange programs could occupy the time of many persons, and we would have no way of knowing this. Items supplied, however, were selected on the basis of preliminary interviews and observation, and it is thought they represent a fair sampling of activities.

6. Paul F. Lazarsfeld has given much attention to this methodological question and its application to social research. See, for example, "Problems in Methodology," in Robert K. Merton, Leonard Broom, and Leonard S. Cottrell, Jr. (eds.), *Sociology Today* (New York: Basic Books, 1959), pp. 47–67. Factor analysis, of course, is one way of identifying clusters of attributes and the dimensions underlying them.

7. Teske, *op. cit.*, p. 106.

8. The first of these types of person appears infrequently; not many persons do all things all the time, so to speak. The latter type is commoner, since this consists of people who engage not in these activities but in others, e.g., personal counseling, informal theological discussions with students, as Table 4–1 indicates.

9. Loats in Earnshaw, *op. cit.*, pp. 301–302.

10. The sources cited in Notes 3 and 4 describe these and other innovative ministries.

11. "Almost" because it is apparent that special preparation is a stronger factor than role conception. These findings, incidentally, hold true for both chaplains and university pastors.

12. See, for example, Frederick Rudolph, *The American College and University* (New York: Alfred A. Knopf, 1962), or L. R. Veysey, *The Emergence of the American University* (Chicago: University of Chicago Press, 1965), for histories of these changes.

13. A number of alternative labels for this distinction come to mind. Heterogeneity, for example, is closely related, as is a spate of terms rich in the history of sociological theory: sacred-secular, mechanical-organic, *gemeinschaft-gesellschaft;* community-associational; primary-secondary, etc. As attributes of collectivities rather than individuals, they all contain

the notion that social life differs according to position on the scale. Each selects slightly different phenomena to accent, however, the accent in our measure being the degree of deviation from the "local" outlook of the early Protestant college. Its antithesis is perhaps best caught up in Clark Kerr's neologism "multiversity." *The Uses of the University* (Cambridge: Harvard University Press, 1963). It should be pointed out that the quality of a school is frequently judged on the basis of its cosmopolitanism, more often in the case of graduate than undergraduate education. No such judgment is necessarily implied in the index here, however. One of the many praiseworthy features of Kerr's essay is the fact that he keeps clearly separate the question of the "nature" of the university from the "uses" to which it might be put.

14. Only 31 cases were classified in the extreme cosmopolitan category, and therefore they have been combined with the adjacent category. The result is six rather than seven groups of schools.

15. See above, p. 75.

5

RESPONSES TO THE
CAMPUS MINISTRY

A number of forces impinge on the campus ministry, as we have just seen in tracing the effects of role conception, preparation, and cosmopolitanism on the styles of campus clergymen. It is now fairly clear why some campus ministers are innovative while others remain traditional in conduct. We understand something about *who* innovates and in *what circumstances*. Investigation of various styles of ministry, however, also raises a correlative issue of responses to campus ministers. How are they received by university and church?

The present chapter pursues this correlative question. First, we provide a framework with which to assess responses to the campus ministry. And second, we identify the reactions of the campus on the one hand and of the denomination on the other.

THE ABSENCE OF ROLE CONFLICT

The role of the campus minister, placed as it is between religion and higher education, might be viewed as a vulnerable candidate for "role conflict," a situation in which contradictory demands meet. Colleges and universities could hold certain expectations of campus clergy, and denominations could hold certain opposing expectations. The campus minister, recognizing the legitimacy of both sets of expectations but unable to conform to both, would experience the result as conflict. Insofar as the situation would be endemic to the position and not a function of happenstance or personality, the problem properly could be called role conflict. Whoever occupied the role of campus minister would be subject to the experience.

But role conflict is not a strategic problem in the campus ministry. Before there can be conflict, there must be the potential for disapproval, and campus ministers are seldom disapproved. Stated in broader terms, before there can be conflicting expectations there must be expectations—and not many people hold expectations of the campus minister.

The evidence is convincing. Respondents were asked: "Assuming the following groups would give an evaluation of your work, indicate as best you can whether each group below would in general tend to be favorable, neutral, or unfavorable toward your campus ministry." The proportion indicating approval ranged from 86 per cent in the case of "denominational officials" to 22 per cent in the case of "students not from active church background." More significant for the discussion of role conflict, however, is the almost total lack of disapproval felt by campus clergy (see Table 5-1). By this measure, very few campus ministers perceive disapproval by any of the groups they more commonly deal with. Where approval is not forthcoming, in other words, neutrality is the observed response.

On other evidence, the conclusion is much the same. The questionnaire inquired whether the respondent felt he was criticized by the university, and by the denomination, for a number of specific things. It asked: "In your opinion, does your college faculty or administration [your denomination

TABLE 5-1.

Evaluating Group	Per Cent of Campus Ministers Reporting That Most of the Group Tend Toward Unfavorable View
College administration	4
Faculty *	2
Students from active church background	2
	2
Students not from active church background	7
Your denominational officials	2
Parish clergy in your denomination	5
Parishioners in your denomination	3

* Asked separately for natural-science, social-science, and humanities faculty. Since the pattern is the same for all three, humanities faculty is used as representative in this and subsequent tables.

(for example, officials, staff, parish clergy)] ever imply these criticisms of you?" Persons could respond with: (1) Yes, many of them probably regard me this way; (2) Yes, this may be true of some, but most would not say this of me; or (3) I have not sensed this attitude on their part.

The great majority (from 47 per cent to 80 per cent with an average of 65 per cent) reported they sensed no criticism in each case. The proportions who thought many criticized them could not, therefore, be great. (See Table 5-2.) Even specific criticisms, in other words, are a rarity in the campus ministry. Equally to the point, when asked further how much such criticisms caused them concern, only 3 per cent allowed that they were concerned "quite a bit." Criticism or disapproval is simply not a significant feature of the campus ministry.[1]

TABLE 5–2.

	PER CENT REPORTING THAT MANY PROBABLY ARE CRITICAL
CRITICISM BY THE COLLEGE	
Drain student energy from course work	3
Not committed enough to the intellectual life	4
Too active in church affairs and meetings	4
Raise too many issues about the purpose of education	7
Too "denominational" in your religious outlook	8
CRITICISM BY THE DENOMINATION	
Encourage students to leave the church	4
Not committed enough to the ministry	5
Not loyal enough to the denomination—too "ecumenical"	15
Too intellectual	17
Not active enough in denominational issues and meetings	14

But if criticism and thus possible conflict are not forces in the campus ministry, indifference is. Campus clergy do not contend with mutually excluding expectations so much as with the *absence* of expectations.

Indifference renders evaluation meaningless. Where approval and disapproval refer to the *direction* of sentiment, indifference and acknowledgment refer to the *amount* of sentiment invested in the evaluation. If the amount of sentiment is small enough, then the direction of sentiment is irrelevant. Campus ministers variously suffer from the indifferent reactions of university and denominations. The degree to which these two spheres acknowledge them varies enormously.

UNIVERSITY ACKNOWLEDGMENT

In the absence of approval, "neutrality" rather than disapproval is the likely response of administration, faculty, and students. Rossman, for instance, investigated state university policies regarding university pastors. On the basis of correspondence with administrators in 48 schools, he declared:

Since the replies record an almost unanimous conclusion that "these clergymen perform a valuable function within our university community," "have worked very cooperatively with the university," and "have contributed greatly to raising the morale and intellectual standards of the student body," it is interesting to note the way in which these questionnaire returns reveal an almost embarrassing lack of policy with reference to denominational chaplains. "We have not thought to examine this question" or "We have not yet formulated any official policy" are typical answers.[2]

A pamphlet on the Methodist college chaplain expresses much the same thought: "Bishops and district superintendents report that only rarely have college presidents taken the initiative to discuss with them the philosophy the college is pursuing in campus ministry or the work of chaplain." [3]

But the indifference or lack of acknowledgment expressed by these situations is not universal. Campus ministerial contexts are widely divergent in this regard, a variable reflecting the degree to which the university knows of the religious ministry being conducted in its midst. To measure this, we asked respondents: "Some people are likely not to know very much about what your campus ministry entails. In general, how much would you say the following persons are *aware of or know* what you are aiming to do in your ministry— know quite well, know somewhat, know little or nothing?" The questionnaire again listed administration, faculty, students from active church background, and students not from active church background. These are four of the more significant university categories with which campus ministers regularly deal; contact with them can hardly be avoided. It becomes reasonable, therefore, to aggregate the perceived knowledge of these four categories and view the result as a measure of the amount of acknowledgment campus ministers receive from their schools. Where all four are seen as "knowing quite well" what he is aiming to do in his ministry, a campus clergyman will feel greatly acknowledged; where all four are seen as "knowing little or nothing," his acknowledgment is low. By assigning 2 points for each "know quite well" answer, 1 point for each "know somewhat" answer, and 0 points for each "know little or nothing," we arrive at a scale of university acknowledgment with scores ranging from 0 to 8. A score of 4 is equivalent to everyone's knowing "somewhat," though there are, of course, several ways to achieve a score of 4 (see Table 5–3).

TABLE 5–3.

Score		Number of Cases
0	Least university acknowledgment	25
1		58
2		151
3		233
4		221
5		140
6		70
7		44
8	Most university acknowledgment	20
	Failed to answer one or more questions	35
	TOTAL	997

Though very few campus ministers score at either extreme, considerable variation exists among respondents in the degree of university acknowledgment they report. This variation is easily detected in the interview comments. One university pastor, for example, said:

> Our job is seen by this university as one pretty much on the outside. They do not provide us with the summer addresses of entering students, so our work is complicated by the fact that we have no access to these students before they actually arrive here. We are not permitted to use university facilities. There has been no clearly articulated policy regarding the religious work in the university, so one gets as many interpretations of it as people he talks to, whether the registrar, dean of admissions, or president's office. This has the effect of saying to students, "Your religious convictions and expressions and experiences are not truly relevant to the life of this university but are something apart from it."

On the same campus, another university pastor put it this way in his interview:

> Students are almost inhibited from coming to the campus minister—by the atmosphere generated at this school, by the standoffishness. So we go out to them, though I definitely feel a barrier every time I go. I am here and the university is there, and little two-way traffic crosses University Avenue. The school doesn't open up its arms and say come in; they are afraid in some measure.

These comments reflect low university acknowledgment. "No access," "no clearly articulated policy," "not truly relevant," and "stand-offish atmosphere" convey a problem not of conflict but of indifference. Contrast the comments of a chaplain at a large private university:

> It is clear to me that the University administration takes very seriously my own appointment as chaplain, associate professor of religion, and coordinator of religious affairs. I have no feeling that I am a fifth wheel of the administrative machine or that I am trotted out for state occasions as a bit of window dressing. I serve on a variety of committees in the University,

and these are regarded as reasonably important in the development of the work of the University.

These remarks, though still devoid of a strong evaluative component, indicate a high degree of acknowledgment from the university. In the first two cases, there was no sign of disapproval or criticism, just indifference; in this last case, the university quite obviously acknowledges the presence of the campus minister. Why this variety of responses?

COSMOPOLITANISM AND UNIVERSITY ACKNOWLEDGMENT

University acknowledgment does not occur at random. It is very much a function of cosmopolitanism. Indifference is more often felt by campus ministers in large public or private universities whose student bodies contain fewer Protestants, as Table 5–4 indicates.

TABLE 5–4.

COSMOPOLITANISM	PER CENT SCORING HIGH (4–8) ON UNIVERSITY ACKNOWLEDGMENT
Very cosmopolitan	38
Quite cosmopolitan	43
Somewhat cosmopolitan	50
Somewhat local	49
Quite local	69
Very local	78

Though not indicated in these figures, the average acknowledgment score for chaplains is regularly higher than for university pastors. Furthermore, cosmopolitanism has less impact on the acknowledgment scores of chaplains. Both of these facts no doubt stem from chaplains' being administratively designated. Apart from such considerations, however, the relationship is unmistakable—with cosmopolitanism comes the increased likelihood that campus ministers will feel more indifference or experience less acknowledgment from the university.

Actually, this relationship is the expected one, as the discussion of the last chapter indicates. The further removed from the Protestant small-college model a school is, the less "automatic" a Protestant clergyman's reception will be. Criticisms from the college are few, as we saw above, but those few are more often felt by campus clergy in cosmopolitan schools. Disapproval of the religious ministry by the academic community is practically nonexistent, as we also saw, but the withholding of approval or reaction of neutrality is commoner in cosmopolitan schools.[4]

OTHER FACTORS INFLUENCING UNIVERSITY ACKNOWLEDGMENT

Cosmopolitanism is not the only factor influencing university acknowledgment. Among chaplains and university pastors, whether on local or cosmopolitan campuses, those who see their educational philosophy [5] as typical of the faculty's educational philosophy are more likely to report higher university acknowledgment than those who see themselves as more conservative or more liberal than the faculty. Similarly, those who regularly read more of the secular magazines the questionnaire asked about are less likely to report indifference from the university, though the number of religious magazines read is unrelated to acknowledgment. It is as though similarity of values, as reflected in educational philosophy and reading habits, enhances a campus minister's sense of reception by the school.

More important than value similarity, however, are a set

of "exposure" variables. Scores increase with the following factors:

1. length of time a school has had a formal campus ministry.
2. amount of formal recognition (in the form of a campus telephone listing, regular channel to the administration, permission to march in academic processions) given a campus minister.
3. frequency with which campus activities (for example, public lectures, athletic events, dances, and so on) are attended by a campus minister.
4. frequency with which a campus minister is called in by the administration for consultation.
5. amount of student participation in campus religious organizations.

All of these factors operate separately for chaplains and university pastors, and in local and cosmopolitan schools. The more contact with campus personnel, the more acknowledgment from them the campus minister reports. The fact that increased exposure brings increased acknowledgment suggests that the measure is not simply campus ministerial "projection" but may indeed reflect the true state of university "reception."

All of these relationships, then, lend support to the interpretation given of the measure of acknowledgment. The problem of the campus minister is one of "entry," of overcoming indifference. And this problem is greater in cosmopolitan schools because "exposure" and "entry" are more difficult there.

COSMOPOLITANISM, ACKNOWLEDGMENT, AND STYLE

Is it any wonder, given these conditions, that the campus ministry in the cosmopolitan setting more often responds (as we observed in Chapter 4) with innovative activities? Traditional, pastoral methods come to be seen as needing overhaul. One university pastor, faced with indifferent responses from a cosmopolitan school, said in an interview:

> This pastoral—or shepherd and flock—pattern is the traditional one, but frankly it can be a very undesirable kind of contact. It can work against the end we are trying to advance, and it can be considered an invasion of students' privacy. Alternatively, by working with a responsible few we can hope that they will become agents among the campus community at large.

A chaplain expresses the indifferent reaction to his ministry in another way:

> The president gives me great freedom. At least there has been no opposition from his office. Maybe we haven't set off enough dynamite to draw a reaction. I don't know. My problem here has been in trying to get students to take on this kind of controversy. There is the real resistance.

From another perspective also—that of a faculty member who for years has been interested in campus religious work—the pastoral methods can be futile. In an interview he stated:

> Some campus ministers fail because they haven't really understood what the university is about. They don't join the inquiry. They should be in the community, wander around and make friends. Instead of trying to draw people off, they should come in, not to oppose what anybody is doing or suppose they have to defend Christianity. The attempts I've seen at apologetics in the university have largely been failures. A good campus minister is devoted to the faculty as well as students, but he can't influence everybody. For example, I have responsibility for about 100 students a year, meeting them three times a week, plus conferences. Of these I can really know perhaps 30 or 40 each year. Now if you put in a campus minister and expect him to have this kind of influence on the whole university that a teacher may have with 30 or 40 students—this would be mad, just mad.

If one source of innovative styles in the campus ministry is clearly the cosmopolitanism of higher education, however, the impact of style on university acknowledgment is equally incontrovertible: It matters not at all. There can be no doubt that innovative and pastoral styles involve different activities; that is the way style is defined and measured. That innovative and pastoral campus ministers differ in the number and nature of their contacts also seems beyond dispute. And there is lots of room to quarrel over which style is more "effective"; disagreement can exist about which pattern does more to further its own aims in higher education. But, according to campus ministers themselves, the *aggregated* knowledge by administration, faculty, and students of the campus ministry is influenced not one bit by differences in style. Innovative campus clergymen, it is true, are perhaps more likely than their traditional colleagues to perceive "students *not* from active church background" as knowing more what their ministry is aiming to do. But the pastoral in style make up the difference with students who *are* from active church background. On local campuses, innovative styles have a slight edge with the faculty, but traditional styles make up for it with the administration.

An academic community, by its cosmopolitanism then, partly determines the style of its campus ministers. And the responses of its various segments may differ depending upon what that style is. But in the *sum* of its acknowledgment, and thus in the extent to which it understands the campus clergy in its midst, a college or university apparently ignores whether the style is pastoral or innovative.

The same can hardly be said of the denomination.

DENOMINATIONAL ACKNOWLEDGMENT

The university context is not the only significant context for campus ministers. As representatives of the church, they also have regular contact with persons in their denomination: officials, parish clergy, and parishioners. We saw above that these categories of people, like those in the university, generally "approve" of the campus ministry. But, in the absence of approval, neutrality—not criticism and disapproval—is their typical response. Acknowledgment from the denomination, then, is also problematic in the campus ministry.

A mild commentary on the lack of acknowledgment comes from this chaplain:

> I have not found any repercussions coming from the denomination. The church doesn't generally become aware of what we do unless some student writes home and complains. One gets letters on occasion from pastors about this, but I've found them sympathetic, more often asking for accurate reports than offering criticisms.

Somewhat stronger is this chaplain's comment:

> The denomination kind of gives up on us characters who are out of the mainstream of the parish ministry. And this is understandable since their meetings are primarily concerned with the business of parishes and programs affecting parish life. A lot of what goes on is not pertinent to my ministry. The people who are least able to understand my absence from those meetings are men who have had no contact with a college minister. The church is not nearly enough aware of the problems of the campus ministry.

On occasion, a campus minister confronts directly the problem of acknowledgment. One university pastor periodically goes

> out into local churches to interpret the work of the foundation. This has gone on since the mid-1950s, trying to educate our people as to what we try to do. Thus, we have minimized the criticism which might otherwise have arisen because of a lack of understanding.

But perhaps the following university pastor's analysis is more typical:

> Those of us in the campus ministry feel that local parishes don't

understand us, and we're sure that we don't really understand the local church. We get together at our conferences and say how nobody loves us—the university doesn't love us, and the church looks at us suspiciously, like we are a beatnik ministry.

One chaplain wrote on the margin of his questionnaire at the point where he could have indicated criticisms from his church, "I am little more than a name on the books of my denomination."

The same procedure used to measure university acknowledgment can be applied to denominational officials, parish clergy, and parishioners, about whom it was asked "In general, how much would you say they are aware of or know what you are aiming to do in your ministry?" Two points were assigned for each "know quite well" response, 1 point for each "know somewhat," and 0 points for "know little or nothing." The result is an index ranging from 0 to 6 (see Table 5–5).

TABLE 5–5.

Score		Number of Cases
0	Least denominational acknowledgment	48
1		105
2		251
3		288
4		167
5		88
6	Most denominational acknowledgment	23
Failed to answer one or more questions		27
TOTAL		997

As in the case of university acknowledgment, what little disapproval there is from the denomination is felt almost exclusively by those scoring very low (0–1) on denominational acknowledgment. Only 1 or 2 per cent of the others indicate disapproval from any source in the church. The situation with criticism is much the same. Specific criticisms [6] of campus ministers are not very common, but they occur more frequently among those scoring low on denomination acknowledgment. Only among the few campus ministers with scores of 0 are all five criticisms very prominent, though none of the five is reported by more than 40 per cent. And only among those with scores lower than 3 is *any* criticism felt by more than 14 per cent. These findings substantiate the discussion with which this chapter began: Some campus clergymen enjoy knowledgeable approval by their denominations and some others experience disapproval without acknowledgment, but the majority get a reaction of indifference. We turn next to the question of why this is the case.

STYLES AND DENOMINATIONAL ACKNOWLEDGMENT

Given the nature of the criticisms from the denomination that campus ministers do feel, it is not surprising that innovative styles evoke less acknowledgment than pastoral styles (see Table 5–6).

TABLE 5–6.

STYLE	PER CENT SCORING HIGH (3–6) ON DENOMINATIONAL ACKNOWLEDGMENT
Most innovative	35
Quite innovative	47
Somewhat innovative	54
Mixed	54
Somewhat pastoral	68
Quite pastoral	75
Most pastoral	79

The penalty for being innovative is obviously great. The proportion who perceive at least a moderate amount of acknowledgment from various categories in the church drops from seven or eight in ten of the most pastoral to three or four in ten of the very innovative. As one university pastor puts it:

> A real problem is the serious mistrust on the part of local churches of the university ministry, a problem related to the church's understanding its mission. It has been so long cast in the role of teacher and defender of morality that it has difficulty conceiving of itself as anything other than this.

"I think perhaps the ministers of some churches are a bit distrustful of us eggheads," says one chaplain. "I'm sure my own denomination," says another, "tends to view me as beyond the pale." It can also be pointed out that chaplains regularly report less denominational acknowledgment than university pastors. Earlier, we saw that the chaplaincy, being college designated, is more acknowledged by the school than is the university pastorate. Now we observe the compensation received by university pastors; they enjoy higher denominational acknowledgment.

OTHER FACTORS INFLUENCING DENOMINATIONAL ACKNOWLEDGMENT

Again, as with acknowledgment from the university, a single factor does not explain all the variation in denominational acknowledgment. Once more, other factors also having impact can be summarized in terms of value similarity on the one hand, exposure or contact variables on the other hand.

For example, among innovative and pastoral alike, in either the university pastorate or chaplaincy, denominational acknowledgment increases with:

(1) desire to see campus ministers more active in their denominations' affairs.

(2) unwillingness to retain an atheist on the faculty of a church-related school (or a publicly supported school).

(3) infrequency of taking stands disapproved by the denomination.

In addition to these value-similarity variables, exposure variables also influence denominational acknowledgment. Scores, for example, increase with:

(1) frequency of contact with parish clergy in the area.

(2) involvement in denomination's regional or national meetings on matters other than the campus ministry.

(3) having more contact with students of one's own denomination.

(4) spending leisure time with parish clergy or friends in the church, rather than faculty, administration, other campus ministers, or other friends.

All of these relationships lend support to the interpretation given of the measure of denominational acknowledgment. Another problem of the campus minister, in other words, is that of gaining or retaining the understanding of his denomination. The more his values differ from those of his denomination's officials, parish clergy, and parishioners, the less acknowledgment from them he will perceive. And the less his involvement, formal or informal, in the denomination's affairs, the more difficulty he has in anticipating their support.[7]

Why should this be the situation? It is not enough merely to relabel the lack of acknowledgment as "distrust" or as "misunderstanding." The question is why do some campus ministers feel their denominations distrust or misunderstand them. Perhaps the key is contained in the comments of one university pastor:

Protestants don't want education; they want indoctrination. Whenever the campus ministry [engages in] study at the collegiate level and begins to produce small numbers of educated and independent laymen, the annual conference (synod, and so forth) gets upset because we are not reaching enough people (quantity not quality is the standard), giving students what they like (more boy-girl relationships and problem-oriented programming typical of the Youth Fellowship), and the students we do affect often question the motives and functions of the church.[8]

Another university pastor said in an interview:

Students begin to ask questions that Sunday-school teachers can't answer, and a lot of them are becoming extremely critical of the church, beginning to ask why the church is not speaking out on certain issues facing society.

Says another:

. . . to anyone who has served both in a local parish and in the more specialized campus ministry, it has often seemed that the latter is regarded by many parish pastors, church officials, and especially church college administrators as a frontier *against* the church rather than a part of its legitimate and urgent mission posture.[9]

If these comments are correct, they suggest that campus ministers are criticized not for what they do, but rather that what they do is seen as critical of the church and therefore is not acknowledged. Passive indifference (the response of cosmopolitan universities) has its parallel here as an active failure to understand. It bears reiteration in this context, however, that conflicting expectations still do not enter—denominations are not saying "Do this" and "Don't do that." Rather, denominations are seen by campus ministers as responding with a plaintive "Why did you do that? We don't understand." The church does not criticize specific acts of its campus clergy so much as it withholds specific approval. The church is not particularly critical of its campus ministry; but it does fail to understand why the campus ministry is critical of it, and therefore refrains from granting acknowledgment.

We have already noted (in Chapter 3) that those with special preparation and differentiated role conceptions are more likely to sound critical of the church. In this chapter, campus ministers with innovative styles, "deviant" values, and minimal contact with their denominations (all associated with special preparation and differentiation) are seen to perceive less acknowledgment from their churches. It is also true that in those denominations (theologically conservative or liturgically oriented) where differentiated conceptions are rare, denominational acknowledgment is higher, but the withdrawing of acknowledgment is also much greater if their campus ministers engage in innovative styles. Conversely, in "liberal" denominations, the penalty for innovation is less, but so is the recognition of the campus ministry generally. The conclusion seems to be this: When campus ministers approximate the traditional role of denominational pastor, they enjoy a feeling of support from the church; when they deviate from that pastoral role, support is withdrawn, to be replaced not with disapproval so much as failure to acknowledge. It is as though their loyalty to the denomination is at issue, and a number of things can call that loyalty into doubt: innovative style, criticizing the denomination, low involvement in church affairs, infrequent contact with parish clergy, and so forth.

If this analysis is correct, then campus ministers whose very positions indicate greater and lesser ties with their denominations should differ in denominational acknowledgment. We have already observed something of this difference in the fact that chaplains are less acknowledged by their denominations than are university pastors. A closer check is possible, however, inasmuch as both chaplaincies and university pastorates vary in the degree to which they are "attached to" denominations.

A chaplaincy may be in a public or private school, in which case the denominational affiliation of its occupant is not specified (though tradition may dictate that it be one or one of several), nor is his affiliation expected to play a prominent part in the execution of his duties. Thus, a Lutheran, say, or an Episcopalian in such a position may feel it necessary to hold "open" communion. In this extreme, perhaps even a chaplain's Protestantism is to be submerged so that Catholic, Jewish, and other students may also have a "chaplain."

Though the situation could be similar for the chaplain of a church-related school, it is less likely. First, a higher proportion of the student body is from a single denomination. And second, the chaplain will almost always be ordained in the church that supports the school (in this study, 91 per cent). The chaplain of a church-related college occupies a position that is more attached to his denomination.

An analogous distinction underlies the university pastorate. The majority, it is true, serve full time in a foundation operated by a single denomination. Some, however, because they also have pastoral duties outside of higher education (typically as an assistant pastor of a local church), are *more* visibly attached to their denominations. And others, because they serve in interdenominational foundations or have developed a cooperative "focused" ministry involving several denominations, are *less* visibly attached to their denominations.

If this dimension of "attachment" is operative, then denominational acknowledgment should differ according to campus ministers' position, and do so independently of the style the occupant effects. The data indicate clearly that such is the case. Though style remains a potent force in denominational acknowledgment, "attachment" of one's position to the denomination also has great impact. Thus, among university pastors with pastoral style, 76 per cent in assistant pastorships report high denominational acknowledgment in contrast to 59 per cent in interdenominational positions. Among those with innovative style, the figures are 59 per cent and 53 per cent. The chaplaincy shows similar differences. Pastoral-style chaplains in church-related schools report a denominational acknowledgment of 64 per cent; those in public or private schools, 54 per cent. The comparable figures for innovative-style chaplains are 43 per cent and 25 per cent. Campus ministers, then, systematically differ in denominational acknowledgment just as they systematically differ in university acknowledgment.

ACKNOWLEDGMENT FROM TWO SPHERES

Those campus ministers who perceive greater acknowledgment from their universities are more likely to perceive greater denominational acknowledgment also (see Table 5–7).

TABLE 5–7.

UNIVERSITY ACKNOWLEDGMENT	PER CENT WITH HIGH (3–6) DENOMINATIONAL ACKNOWLEDGMENT
Low score 0–1	29
2	44
3	62
4	59
5	77
6	71
High score 7–8	78

Far from indicating a Panglossian effect, however, this relationship results from a paradox in the campus ministry that can now be made explicit. Campuses responding with indifference to the Protestant ministry in their midst are more cosmopolitan campuses. These schools, because they are cosmopolitan and because their campus ministers have more specialized training and differentiated role conceptions, evoke more innovation in chaplains and university pastors. And churches respond to innovation with decreased acknowledgment—their own kind of indifference. Conversely, campus ministers who experience fewer pressures to innovate enjoy, as a corollary to those fewer pressures, greater university acknowledgment. But in addition, by virtue of not innovating, they also enjoy greater denominational acknowledgment. In other words, campus clergymen most in need of support from one source because support is not forthcoming from another source are precisely the ones who are least likely to receive it.

The paradox may operate differently for different campus ministers. Because of ambivalence toward the church, some elect a campus ministry as far from the denomination as possible. The result: Reduced denominational support for work in a post at a cosmopolitan school with reduced university support. Other campus ministers may find themselves in an indifferent atmosphere and react with innovative style. The result: Reduced denominational support because of their response to reduced university support. For others, the paradox operates still another way; the more cosmopolitan campuses have much the higher proportion of interdenominational university pastorates, just as public and private college chaplaincies will, as a rule, be located on more cosmopolitan campuses. The result: Occupants of these positions experience reduced denominational support because their "attachment" to the church is less, and they experience reduced university support because they are in cosmopolitan schools.

Regardless of the path of the paradox, however, the result is identical. Some campus clergymen are caught in a complex of factors making their work almost self-defeating, just as others enjoy a receptive location arising from equally complex factors. Noting this double-contingency nature of the campus ministerial role, Earnshaw says:

> The lines of responsibility for campus ministry extend . . . to the church and . . . to the university. . . . The campus minis-

ter stands in a place of mediation. He must be sensitive to both directions and, in a sense, is held accountable by both.[10]

As we have seen, campus ministers *are* sensitive to both directions, though whether this sensitivity helps or hinders depends upon a number of things. We continue this question in the next chapter.

NOTES

1. A certain parallelism will be noted in the criticisms listed above. For example, the college might say "not intellectual enough" or "too denominational" and the church might say "too intellectual" or "too ecumenical." The research was planned in a way designed to uncover evidence of role conflict, but with so few respondents reporting that they felt criticized, it became apparent that role conflict (at least in its usual sense of contradictory expectations) was not a key to understanding the campus ministerial occupation. We are not saying, of course, that individual campus clergymen never feel criticized but only that criticism is not a socially structured part of their role. An individual who experiences it may have little idea whether criticism is personal and idiosyncratic or patterned and structured. One advantage of survey research, it might be said in passing, is to provide information for distinguishing the two.
2. Parker Rossman, "The Denominational Chaplain in the State University," *Religious Education*, LV (1960), 5.
3. *The Methodist College Chaplain*, p. 11.
4. Indeed, as further evidence of the unimportance of role conflict in understanding the campus ministry, it can be pointed out that only two persons (out of 997) indicated that there were university personnel who both knew "quite well" and "disapproved of" their ministry. In other words, indifferent approval is the general reaction, though now we see that indifferent neutrality is oftener the response of the cosmopolitan school.
5. See above, pp. 46–47.
6. See above, pp. 86–87.

7. It is important to remember that the measures of acknowledgment by university and denomination are measures of *perceived* support. We are using campus ministers' *reports* of others' knowledge of their ministry. The fact that both scores increase with increased exposure to church and college *suggests* that the measures may reflect "reality" and not just the personal perceptions of respondents, but this fact does not *prove* the case. In any event, if campus ministers' behavior is what is being explained, the world as they see it is the relevant world.

8. D. R. Ploch, letter to the editor, *Christianity and Crisis,* XXII (1962), 115.

9. Myron M. Teske in Earnshaw (ed.), *The Campus Ministry,* pp. 102–103.

10. Earnshaw, *op. cit.,* pp. 32–34.

PART III

PART III

6

INSTITUTIONALIZATION

OF THE CAMPUS MINISTRY

We have observed a paradoxical consequence of the interplay of two spheres: As higher education becomes more cosmopolitan, it withdraws acknowledgment of the campus ministry at the same time it evokes innovative style. To innovative style, however, the denomination responds by reducing its acknowledgment. This situation at least is the campus ministerial *experience;* campus clergymen who perceive indifference on the one side are also likely to perceive indifference (if not criticism) on the other side, though the sources of the two types of indifference are different.

ACKNOWLEDGMENT AND CLARITY
IN OWN POSITION

It is appropriate to ask, therefore, whether campus ministers' interstitial position makes their *own* sense of clarity in the role vulnerable to university and denominational indifference. This role clarity is the same phenomenon discussed in

Chapter 1. It is measured by respondents' answers to the question: "Some observers have noted a lack of specificity in campus ministerial duties. They say that a man coming to a new position has little idea of what is expected of him, and that little agreement exists among others of what he is to do. In short, they say the campus ministry has a vague job description. How accurate a portrayal of your position is this observation?" (See Table 6–1.) The first two answers are con-

TABLE 6–1.

Very accurate. My position is vaguely defined	17%
Quite accurate. My position is not very clearly defined	36
Not very accurate. My position is quite clearly defined	35
Inaccurate. My position is very clearly defined	12
	100%

sidered indicative of ambiguity; the last two answers, indicative of a sense of clarity. Table 6–2 shows the proportion of campus ministers reporting a sense of clarity under varying conditions of university and denominational acknowledgment.

It is obvious from Table 6–2 that campus ministers' own sense of clarity is contingent upon, or at least related to, the degree to which they perceive others in the university and denomination as having knowledge of their campus ministry. It could hardly be otherwise, if respondents are accurate reporters. In the question concerning the clarity-ambiguity in their own position, they were asked in part about the "agreement among others" of what is expected of campus ministers. Without knowledge, there cannot be agreement of expectations; to be consistent, a respondent perceiving low acknowledgment by others would have to report less agreement by them and thus less clarity in his own role. The latter is contingent upon both spheres.

TABLE 6–2. *Clarity of Campus Ministerial Position under Varying Conditions of University and Denominational Acknowledgment*

		PER CENT WHOSE POSITION IS CLEAR WHEN DENOMINATIONAL ACKNOWLEDGMENT IS				
	Score	Low 0–1	2	3	4	High 5–6
	Low 0–1	27 (22)	35 (37)	* 38 (24)	*	†
UNIVERSITY ACKNOWLEDG-MENT IS	2–3	28 (58)	36 (116)	34 (138)	49 (45)	70 (23)
	4	37 (24)	40 (65)	45 (65)	58 (40)	48 (23)
	5–6	43 (37)	52 (23)	62 (55)	67 (55)	67 (36)
	High 7–8	* 77	* (13)	* 71	* (21)	75 (24)

* Adjacent cells collapsed because of few cases.
† Vacant cell.

One university pastor expresses very well the "dual-contingency" nature of his position:

> Here on this campus our nebulous position, both in ecclesiastical relationships as well as our peripheral relationship to the university because of state regulations, leaves us men without a country. This is not true of campus ministers in some areas. They can be more effective by having some image—be it good or bad—by having *some* relationship to both the church and the university.

More than the double contingency of campus ministers' own role clarity is indicated in Table 6–2, however. Though the evidence is small because the relevant cases are few, it appears that very high acknowledgment from even one source (university *or* denomination) is sufficient to produce a rate of clarity at or near the maximum. Thus, all the cells (with one exception, for which we have no explanation) across the bottom row and down the right-hand column contain high percentages. It is as though some minimum acknowledgment score is necessary before a certain level of clarity is reached; after that minimum is met (whether from one or both spheres), then added increments of acknowledgment do not have a commensurate effect on clarity. On the scales used in Table 6–2, this point would seem to be approximately a score of 8.[1]

Actually, a total score of 8 does have a special significance in these measures. The two acknowledgment scales are based on seven categories of persons (role partners), with points of 2, 1, and 0 assigned to answers for each category knowing "quite well," "somewhat," or "little or nothing" about the respondent's aims in his ministry. A total score of 8, then, means that at least one of the seven role partners is seen as knowing "quite well" what the respondent's ministry is about. If we ignore whether the role partners' locations are in university or church and observe only the total acknowledgment score, this hypothesis receives some support. The proportion of campus ministers reporting their own position to be clear hovers around one-third up through a total score of 6, though there are small and rather consistent increases from a score of 0 to a score of 6. A score of 7 has associated with it a rate of 47 per cent. But of respondents with a score of 8 or 9, the proportion indicating clarity in their own role is about 60 per cent, and the proportion clear among those with scores of 10 to 14 (maximum) is at least two-thirds.

It is possible, of course, to exaggerate the symbolic importance of a single score. Certainly no exaggeration is meant here. But the "natural break," if it is more than coincidence, does support the contention that one's own sense of clarity in a role is contingent on the degree to which relevant other persons are seen as knowing what that role entails. It is true, moreover, that only a few respondents report very high acknowledgment from one sphere but very low acknowledgment from the other; most persons with a score higher than 6 or 8 are therefore perceiving at least some acknowledgment from role partners in both church and university.

TENURE, ACKNOWLEDGMENT, AND CLARITY

Campus ministers' own role clarity is not contingent solely on others' degree of knowledge, but the latter's importance far outweighs the importance of other factors. Tenure, for example, the length of time a person has held his position, has some impact on his own sense of clarity. But with the level of acknowledgment held constant, the impact is rather slight.

The data indicate that experience in a position carries with it a greater likelihood of high acknowledgment (27 per cent of persons in their first or second year have scores of 8 or higher in contrast with 40 per cent of those with six or more years in a position). But independent of this increased acknowledgment, experience adds only slight increments to clarity. The probable exception is among persons with medium acknowledgment, the "borderline" cases discussed above. Being on the borderline between low and high acknowledgment, they are seemingly in a situation where experience alone can significantly enhance their own sense of clarity as campus clergy. This is not so with others, however. Among those with low acknowledgment, even veterans of six or more years have only slightly more clarity than neophytes; and among those enjoying high acknowledgment, neophytes have only slightly less clarity than veterans.[2] Once again the possibility of a natural breaking point in acknowledgment is observed: Those with scores of 6 or lower are likely to be in "vague" positions irrespective of experience; those with scores of 8 or higher are likely to be in "clear" positions irrespective of experience.

DEGREE OF POSITIONAL DEFINITION

So we return to a discussion begun in Chapter 1—the effects, or at least the correlates, of being in a position that may be well defined—or poorly defined. This time, however, the complex of factors producing in occupants their own degree of clarity is known. A person coming into a campus ministerial post will find that, depending upon (1) the cosmopolitanism of the campus, (2) his exposure or contact with it and with his denomination, and (3) the style of his own ministry, the various persons relevant to his work will differ in how well they "acknowledge" his ministry. At best, all of these other persons will know quite well what he, as a campus minister, is trying to do, and he will likely find his own execution of the role to be clear. At the other extreme, other persons will know little or nothing of his aims; they will be "indifferent," and he will look upon his role as vague.

It seems reasonable to consider as clearest positions those which are greatly acknowledged by others *and* whose occupants also are clear about their work. Conversely, least clear are those positions about which *neither* occupants nor others are clear. These two kinds of position represent the extremes in degree of "definition." In between are positions with varying degrees of definition, depending upon how well the occupants and others know the positions. A measure of degree of definition—we shall call it positional definition—is possible using the acknowledgment scores (0–6; 7; 8–9; 10–14) and campus ministers' responses to the question of their own clarity (very vague; vague; clear; very clear). The highest positional definition is assigned, thus, to those who report an acknowledgment score of 10–14 and who report they are "very clear" about their own role. The lowest positional definition is assigned to those who have an acknowledgment score of 0–6 and who are also "very vague" about their own role.

On occasion, because of fewer cases at either extreme, the resulting seven categories will be collapsed into fewer, but first we can observe some of the differences among campus ministers varying greatly in positional definition.

A significant difference associated with positional definition, for example, might be regarded as one of "tone." Those in well-defined positions have greater *elan* or zest for the campus ministry. Indicating something of this difference are answers to the following questions:

1. How satisfied are you with the quality of student most attracted to your ministry?
2. How often do you have doubts about your work, question your effectiveness, or wonder why you're in this profession anyway?
3. How often do you feel a sense of accomplishment, experience a fullness or sense of well-being, or feel grateful that you're in this vocation?
4. Taking all the features of your position into account, how much do you enjoy your work?

In each case, positional definition is related to the way campus ministers answer. Thus, 66 per cent of those persons in least defined positions are "quite satisfied" with the quality of their students, but this figure increases with increased definition to 90 per cent of those in most defined positions. Thirty-one per cent of the former have "frequent doubts" about their work, but only 7 per cent of the latter report such frequent doubts. A "sense of accomplishment" is frequently felt by 43 per cent at the one extreme, by 72 per cent at the other. And finally, 30 per cent in least defined positions, but 52 per cent in most defined positions, "cannot think of work they would enjoy as much."

Quite obviously, positional definition is related to the pleasure and enjoyment campus ministers may experience. Positional definition, not surprisingly, therefore, is also related to campus ministers' self-evaluation. Respondents were asked to indicate briefly their understanding of the purpose of the campus ministry, after which they were asked:

1. Taking all things into account, how close does your ministry come to fulfilling this purpose?

Later in the questionnaire this question appeared:

2. In comparison with other campus ministers you know, how good a job do you think you are doing?

Those whose positional definition is very or quite high responded in 43 per cent of the cases that they come "quite close" to fulfilling the purpose of the campus ministry. By contrast, only 17 per cent of those whose positional definition is very or quite low gave that optimistic response. Answers to the second question are similar: Sixty-one per cent in the better-defined positions report they are "perhaps doing a better job" than most campus ministers; in the poorly defined positions, only 41 per cent gave that answer. Insofar as these respondents are accurate evaluators, we can infer that campus ministerial effectiveness increases with increasing positional definition.

These findings should not come as a surprise. Investigation after investigation finds more or less the same relationship: Ill-defined or ambiguous positions have unpleasant effects for their occupants. For example, in their inventory of propositions about behavior in organizations, March and Simon report that: "In general, and up to a fairly extreme point, increased predictability yields increased satisfaction for most people—particularly in activities that are primarily instrumental." [3] Kahn and his associates, in research on managers and foremen in industrial organizations, found similar results. Their measure of positional ambiguity, furthermore, did not rely (as ours does) on occupants' *perceptions* of others' expectations, but was a composite score of what in fact others knew and expected. They found the individual consequences of being in ambiguous positions to be "low job satisfaction, low self-confidence, a high sense of futility, and a high score on the tension index." [4]

The reasons for these effects on the occupants of poorly defined positions are not difficult to understand. Persons need to be economical with their energy and other resources; the less they have to spend trying to define where they stand and where they are going, the greater their mastery and control over the expenditure of resources. The more certain persons are in their social relationships, the better able they are to budget resources and direct them into creative channels. Feelings of satisfaction and accomplishment, then, are likely products of clearly defined positions, dissatisfaction and doubt likely products of ambiguous positions.

Another correlate of positional definition is the likelihood of staying in the campus ministry. Naturally enough, individuals whose positions contribute to their dissatisfaction and discouragement are also more likely to leave those positions. The questionnaire contained many questions which, in different ways, asked if the respondent might leave. In every case, regardless of how the question is asked, the lower the respondents' positional definition, the greater is their predilection to quit. They are more likely, for example, to have "given serious thought to the possibility of leaving" their present position. They more frequently have "taken steps toward moving" from their present position. They have less "intention now of making the campus ministry a life-long career." And their actual one-year turnover rate is greater. At every available opportunity, in other words, respondents in poorly defined positions indicated weaker attachment to those positions. Positional definition is clearly a salient feature of the campus ministry.

SHARED EXPECTATIONS IN THE
CAMPUS MINISTRY

Positional definition is also tantamount to a measure of "shared expectations," one of the two components in the process of institutionalization, discussed in Chapter 2. Several comments therefore can be made about this aspect of institutionalization in the campus ministry:

1. Positions in the campus ministry differ in the degree to which the persons involved (role occupant and role partners) share expectations of the campus clergyman.
2. Shared expectations are more often found on "local" than on "cosmopolitan" campuses, since university acknowledgment is greater on local campuses.
3. Shared expectations are more likely to develop around "pastoral" rather than "innovative" styles of campus ministerial activity, since denominational acknowledgment of pastoral style is greater.

Institutionalization of the campus ministry, on these grounds then, would seem more probable on local campuses on which pastoral-style ministries are being conducted. In the discussion of the "path of institutionalization," however, the argument was advanced that shared expectations must not only be present but also shift from a "borrowed" to an "indigenous" basis. We have reason to believe that pastoral styles on local campuses are unable to make that shift.

There seems to be no question but what the parish or pastoral model was the borrowed model in the campus ministry. We noted in Chapter 1, for example, that many denominations charged their earliest campus clergymen with the duty of transporting the parish to the campus. They were to care for members of their own flocks, and do so largely in the manner of their parish counterparts. Even today, students, faculty, administration, and denominational officials all would describe campus ministers, in the majority of cases, as "pastors" rather than as "teaching ministers" or "religious voices in the academic community." This, at least, is campus ministers' perception, even though only a minority so describe themselves.[5] And the borrowed pattern persists even for some campus clergy. As one university pastor said in an interview:

> In a normal day, a parish minister would spend time studying, preparing sermons, hospital visiting, and so on. This is my job, too, except it is done in the context of the campus.

This person, who reflects little or nothing that is innovative in his ministry, clearly has imported the parish model. Pastoral style is borrowed style.

True, there is no intrinsic reason why borrowed expectations cannot become indigenous. The distinction is based not so much on substantive acts (what persons *do*) as it is based on the appropriateness with which persons regard what is done. The pastoral style, therefore, conceivably could come to be regarded as distinctively appropriate for the ministry to higher education, could, that is, become indigenous.

Several crucial factors prevent pastoral expectations from becoming indigenous expectations, however, as we observed in Chapters 3 and 4. Increasing formal education and specialized preparation tend to produce differentiated role conceptions, and campuses tend to become more cosmopolitan. These changes inhibit pastoral style and encourage innovative style. Hence, the appropriateness of the former is constantly being challenged, which means that, though pastoral expectations presently yield the highest probability of being shared, they are unlikely to become distinctively appropriate. One reason for impeded institutionalization of the campus ministry, therefore, lies in its reduced capacity to shift from borrowed to indigenous shared expectations.

COMMITMENT IN THE
CAMPUS MINISTRY

The second component of institutionalization is "commitment," the extent to which persons involved in an activity regard that activity as justified or important. In Chapter 2 we noted that there must be not only expectations but also commitment to them. We are handicapped at this point by having no measure of role-partners' commitment other than an assessment of their acknowledgment, used already to indicate the *presence* of expectations, but not necessarily *commitment* to them. Neutrality, however, was seen as the dominant response of church and college, appearing sometimes with expectations or acknowledgment and sometimes without. This suggests that more strategic than role-partners' commitment is the commitment of campus clergy themselves. And we do have a very good yardstick of this component, based on the tenacity campus ministers show in wanting to be in the campus ministry. Such a measure requires only the minimal assumption that persons who express, even under adverse conditions, an intention of remaining in the campus ministry are thereby more committed to it. We have already seen how lack of shared expectations (low positional definition) weakens the attachment persons have to their positions. We raise now the correlative question of who weakens first. Why are some campus ministers more committed than others?

The answer is clear cut. Those most committed to the campus ministry, irrespective of the definition of their positions, are persons with specialized training and differentiated role conceptions. Table 6–3 supplies the evidence.

Except for the equivocation of role conception on the commitment of persons in highly defined positions (left-hand column, bottom half of table, this exception will be discussed later), the relationships of Table 6–3 are unmistakable: The

TABLE 6–3. *Within Levels of Positional Definition, the Impact of Specialized Training and Role Conception on Commitment to the Campus Ministry*

		POSITIONAL DEFINITION			
*Per Cent Who Are Definitely or Probably Staying * Among*		*Very or Quite High*	*Somewhat High or Moderate*	*Somewhat Low*	*Very or Quite Low*
	Very high	67 (18)	60 (40)	64 (50)	55 (67)
	High	75 (40)	50 (76)	62 (76)	44 (132)
SPECIAL PREPARATION	Low	63 (24)	51 (74)	46 (61)	33 (98)
	Very low	55 (31)	34 (47)	32 (37)	28 (57)
	Difference =	12	26	32	27
	Much	50 (12)	60 (42)	60 (58)	49 (94)
DEGREE OF DIFFERENTIATION IN ROLE CONCEPTION	Some	61 (18)	54 (52)	60 (53)	40 (90)
	Moderate	63 (27)	50 (44)	59 (46)	36 (91)
	Little	70 (50)	43 (83)	40 (60)	35 (65)
	Difference =	−20	17	20	14

The question wording appears above, p. 14, and is discussed there and on p. 8.

greater the special preparation for the campus ministry and the more differentiated one's conception of it, the greater is the commitment to it. These relationships are indicated in the two rows of differences. Alternatively, we may note that among the undifferentiated in role conception or among those with little specialized preparation, the rate at which they intend to remain in the campus ministry seldom exceeds 50 per cent, even in well-defined positions. Conversely, among those with

differentiated role conceptions and those with high levels of
preparation, the rate of intention to remain seldom drops below 50 per cent, even in poorly defined positions. The commitment of the latter is greater; specialized preparation and
differentiated role conceptions seem to *predispose* clergymen
to remain on campus. The joint effect of the two variables
is stronger than either is singly.[6]

We might have anticipated this finding for two reasons.
First, we observed earlier (Chapter 3) that those with differentiated role conceptions are more "campus ministerial": We
saw that they gave more *reasons* for being campus clergymen,
and that features unique to campus work are more appealing
to them; and we saw that as all campus clergymen differ from
other groups, so are the differentiated distinguished from the
undifferentiated.[7] Second, one of the purposes of specialized
training clearly is to interest trainees in their specialty and
convince them of its importance. By providing seminary
courses, internships, workshops, and specialized literature, and
thus also by encouraging the development of differentiated
role conceptions, churches succeed in committing some campus clergy to the campus ministry.

It is possible to speak of commitment in the campus ministry, therefore, even though, like shared expectations, commitment is variable; some have more than others. But again, however, it is not enough that commitment to the campus ministry
merely be present. The *basis* of this commitment is important,
too, whether borrowed or indigenous. It is important, that
is, for persons to choose the campus ministry not for external
reasons, not because it is like something else or because it is
a pathway to something else, but because the *role* of the campus clergyman is thought important in its own right.

There is little doubt but what the campus ministry has borrowed commitment. In the case of those who define it as little
different from the parish ministry, this borrowed commitment
is fairly clear. Probably the parents, parishioners, church offi-

cials, faculty, and students who fail to understand the aims of innovative campus clergy, and for this reason are critical, are also "committed" to the borrowed model from the parish.[8]

But there are others whose commitment is borrowed. Some observers suggest that the campus ministry draws into it persons who are really aspiring professors, or persons not yet willing to accept the responsibilities of the parish, or persons who are escaping from the church. For example, one national administrator of his denomination's religion-and-higher-education department said in an interview:

> One thing we look out for is a person's attitude toward the institutional church. If he is in complete revolt against it in all its sin, he is of very little help. We do have some fellows who want the campus ministry as an escape from the church. A lot also feel that the way to get into teaching is through the campus ministry.

Says his counterpart in another denomination, "Some haven't quit playing college ball yet, and the campus ministry looks like an opportunity to continue."

The impact of this situation on the institutionalization of the campus ministry depends, of course, upon where it is located. If borrowed commitment occurs chiefly among those who are not likely to remain in the campus ministry anyway, then no inordinate hindrance is created. But if it occurs among those who otherwise are logical candidates for long-term careers as campus clergymen, then strategic barriers to institutionalization appear. The answer is that both situations occur. Some enter the campus ministry with commitment borrowed from the parish sphere, and their weaker attachment represents no *added* factor in the retardation of institutionalization. These would-be preachers, so to speak, are likely to be lost to the campus ministry eventually anyway. Would-be teachers, on the other hand, do represent a socially structured impediment to institutionalization because they appear chiefly among the sector who are predisposed to remain in the campus ministry. Some relevant evidence is found in Table 6–4.

TABLE 6–4. *Predisposition to Remain in the Campus Ministry and Likelihood of Changing to the Parish or to College Teaching*

	PREDISPOSITION TO REMAIN *						
PER CENT OF CAMPUS MINISTERS WHO	Low 0	1	2	3	4	5	High 6
A. Would like to move to the parish	16	15	21	13	10	7	9
B. Would move to the parish if they left present position	35	44	34	23	23	10	11
C. Would like full-time college teaching	16	24	26	26	32	38	33
D. Would move to college teaching if they left present position	23	14	18	27	27	34	31
N =	(75)	(117)	(159)	(188)	(175)	(115)	(55)

* This index is the combination of special preparation (4 categories) and role conception (4 categories) as they appear in Table 6–3. A score of 6 = Very High Preparation plus Much Differentiation; a score of 5 = Very High Preparation plus some Differentiation, *or* Much Differentiation plus High Preparation, and so forth.

Respondents were asked to "indicate how willing you would be to change if you were called from your present position to: (1) full-time college teaching, and (2) parish ministry." For each they answered that they would "change with enthusiasm," "probably like to change," "be willing to change," or "not want to change." The first two answers are taken as indicative of a preference for the job in question over the present job as campus clergyman. In Table 6–4, rows A and C represent the answers of persons classified by their predisposition to remain in the campus ministry. Earlier in the questionnaire, respondents supplied an answer to the open-ended question, "If you were to leave your present position, to what kind of position would you most likely go?" Rows B and D of Table 6–4 contain the percentages of those who volunteered answers of "parish ministry (or church administration)" and "full-time teaching (or college administration)."

As Table 6–4 makes clear, though not very many campus ministers *prefer* the parish over the campus ministry (Row A), a sizable minority would expect to go there should they leave their present positions (Row B). Inasmuch as such persons appear in much greater proportion in the sector which is not predisposed to remain in campus work anyway, they are no *added* barrier to institutionalization. Rows C and D tell a different story, however. It is apparent from these data that the predisposition to remain in the campus ministry is accompanied by a preference for *and a higher probability of entering* full-time teaching. Here is the explanation for the "reversal" noted in one column of Table 6–3; location in well-defined positions does *not* increase the intention to stay of those with differentiated role conceptions, for along with that differentiation may come a commitment or desire to teach. Inasmuch as this is true of a sizable minority, the situation *does* represent an impediment to institutionalizing the campus ministry, because these are precisely the people who most likely could effect a shift in commitment from a borrowed to an indigenous basis. These are the persons whose differentiated role conceptions and specialized training predispose them to remain in the campus ministry, but their commitment is more to the "campus" than it is to the "ministry." [9]

The difference between borrowed and indigenous commitment to the campus ministry is illustrated in the following excerpts from personal interviews. All three persons are committed to the campus ministry, enjoy their work, and are in reasonably well-defined positions. But where the first reveals what we have called an indigenous commitment, the other two reveal a borrowed commitment.

Campus minister A: I wouldn't trade my present job for anything I've been in so far. I wouldn't want college teaching. I did not prepare for it, and I don't enjoy teaching as much as some other aspects of my job. Neither would I want to return to the parish. I don't know what I would do if they didn't want me around here.

Campus minister B: At present I enjoy my work and don't contemplate a change. The work is relevant, and as long as I continue to see evidence that it is, I think I would stay on quite readily. But if I were to leave, right now my interest is in classroom work; that would head my list of preferences—full-time teaching.

Campus minister C: I'm not teaching in order to establish myself on the campus. I teach because that is my calling, the chaplaincy being my second calling. If by the grace of God and the judgment of the administration I should be the chaplain, then I'll continue. But I find the chaplaincy satisfying so long as it has an academic orientation.

Borrowed commitment is reflected also in the Danforth Foundation's fellowship program for campus clergy. Designed to enable recipients of a fellowship to take a year-long leave of absence to study and better equip themselves for careers in the campus ministry, the program has suffered some attrition. Of the 86 persons granted the award in its first five years (1957–61), slightly less than half (46 per cent) are now practicing campus ministers. The next largest proportion (17 per cent) are teaching in college or seminary. The remainder are equally divided among parish ministry (some of these are pastors in college towns), church administration (some of these are administrators of "higher-education" divisions in their denominations), or miscellaneous other fields, including continued study.[10]

Charges of campus ministerial deviousness are not necessarily warranted, nor are they necessary for the point being made here. Whether persons *enter* the occupation with a desire for the parish or teaching, or whether they *arrive at* those motives as a result of the ambiguities in their positions, the fact seems to be that sizable numbers never develop an indigenous commitment to the role of the campus minister. To the extent this failure occurs among those whose predisposition to remain campus ministers is otherwise high, the effect is great. Another reason for impeded institutionalization, therefore, lies in the occupation's reduced capacity to shift from borrowed to indigenous commitment.

CONVERGENCE OF EXPECTATIONS AND COMMITMENT

But just as we have uncovered conditions which impede institutionalization, so also by implication have we discovered facilitating conditions. There *are* positions characterized by shared expectations, some of them accurately described as indigenous. And there *are* persons with commitment to the campus ministry, some of them with indigenous commitment. Are these not the ingredients of an institutionalizing occupational role? As Clark has stated:

> An embryonic profession can be generated only on the basis of favorable work conditions. There must be a corps of full-time workers who are engaged in similar types of work and who are interested in their work as a permanent commitment.[11]

We seem to have discovered some favorable "work conditions" as well as a "corps of workers" committed to their work. Why, then, has institutionalization not developed around these elements?

The answer, of course, and the major barrier to institutionalization, lies in the fact that *the persons predisposed to be committed to the campus ministry are least likely to be in positions marked by shared expectations.* This relationship was implied in Chapters 4 and 5, but if any doubt about it remains, that doubt should disappear with a glance at Table 6–5.

TABLE 6–5. *Predisposition to Remain in the Campus Ministry and Positional Definition, Style, and Cosmopolitanism*

PER CENT OF CAMPUS MINISTERS WHO ARE (HAVE)	PREDISPOSITION TO REMAIN *						
	Low						High
	0	1	2	3	4	5	6
Somewhat, quite, or very low positional definition	39	50	54	64	64	66	76
Innovative in style	17	22	37	48	48	49	58
In cosmopolitan schools	54	54	62	60	75	74	78
N =	(76)	(128)	(172)	(197)	(185)	(122)	(55)

* Slightly higher numbers of cases appear in this table than in Table 6–4 because more persons answered these questions.

The first row of Table 6–5 indicates the clear and positive relationship between the predisposition to remain and the likelihood of being in a poorly defined position. And the next two rows indicate why. Repeating earlier findings in slightly different form, the bottom two rows document again that the features of the campus ministry which hinder the development of shared expectations—innovative style and cosmopolitan campus—are far more characteristic of the very persons most committed to being clergymen on campus. Inasmuch as a low degree of shared expectations weakens the attachment of occupants to their positions, and encourages them to leave, the turnover of personnel remains high throughout the occupation. Those predisposed to stay, because theirs are poorly defined positions, are more likely to leave; and those in well-defined positions, because their commitment is not great, are more likely to leave.

With rapid movement in and out of the role, a "corps of full-time workers" has less chance to develop. The probability remains low that any coherent set of expectations will become *the* expectations defining the role. New generations of campus ministers must therefore contend each time with the problem of "definition"—what they and their role-partners shall expect of them. Any sense of clarity they themselves arrive at will be "private" and not easily passed on to subsequent campus clergymen. The outcome is an occupation characterized by ambiguity and turnover; the latter results from the former, and vice versa. But in addition, both can be viewed as results of disjunctive social structural arrangements—arrangements minimizing the convergence of shared expectations and commitment.

Conclusion

Three empirically related, but analytically separate, reasons have thus been given to explain the campus ministry's failure to institutionalize. Barriers stand in the way of the necessary shift from borrowed to indigenous expectations. Other barriers stand in the way of the necessary shift from borrowed to indigenous commitment. And the social structural arrangements whereby persons are allocated to positions mean that expectations and commitment are least likely to converge. The bulk of this argument, and the variables involved in it, can now be diagrammed (see Figure 6–1). We leave to the last chapter a more detailed summary and identification of possible policy decisions which may compensate for the barriers to institutionalization in the campus ministry.

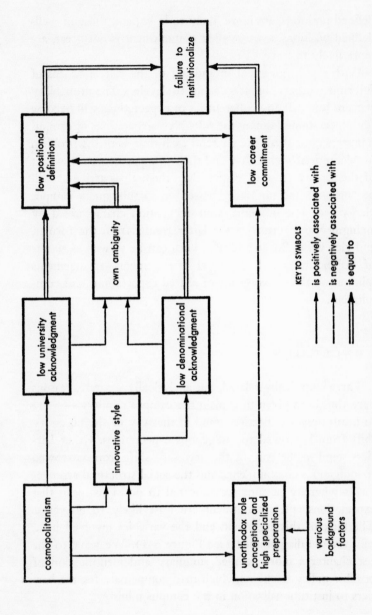

FIGURE 6-1. Diagram of factors accounting for the failure of institutionalization.

NOTES

1. No unwarranted meaning should be applied to a score of 8 or any other number. The scales used are ordinal only; apparent units on those scales are not units in fact. Reasons for the minimum necessary score, therefore, must be theoretical not mathematical.
2. For one-third of the respondents, "present position" is not the first campus ministerial post. Relationships are not changed, however, if calculated separately for those with and without prior campus ministry positions.
3. James March and H. Simon, *Organizations* (New York: Wiley, 1958), p. 94.
4. R. L. Kahn, *et al.*, *Organizational Stress* (New York: Wiley, 1964), p. 380.
5. See p. 53.
6. It might be noted also that the relationships of Table 6–3 hold separately for university pastors and chaplains.
7. See p. 54.
8. See p. 98.
9. If one looks only at respondents in positions at least "moderately well defined" (the cadre in a situation especially crucial in institutionalizing the campus ministry), the percentages in Row C change from the significant 16–33 per cent to 13–46 per cent. Among those whose positional definition is at least "quite high," the percentage range is a remarkable 5–75, though of course the cases are very few.
10. Excluded from these figures are ten persons whose whereabouts are unknown. Recipients of the award since 1961 are not included since their "destinations" are still in flux. More of them, for example, are still in graduate study. (Information supplied by the Danforth Foundation.)
11. Clark, *Adult Education in Transition*, p. 152.

7

RECAPITULATION AND
POLICY IMPLICATIONS

The campus ministry thus far has failed to institutionalize. For a period of six decades, Protestants have conducted a ministry to higher education, but they have not succeeded in establishing a pattern of activity to which persons can easily commit themselves for a lifetime career, and about which there is little ambiguity. However, since the costs of institutionalization include some loss of flexibility and inventiveness, and since frequent responses to ambiguity are innovative thinking and ingenious adjustment, it may be that the sacrifice at these points is considered too costly for the return.

Moreover, the failure to institutionalize has been largely an "internal" failure wherein campus ministers—not others—have paid the larger price. With the possible exception of some chaplaincies, higher education certainly is little concerned about or made uncomfortable by the ambiguity and rapid turnover of campus clergy in its midst. True, higher education may feel benefited by sustained, established campus ministries, but it need not feel handicapped when those ministries lack continuity and establishment. And from the standpoint of whole denominations, just the *presence* of a campus ministry—irrespective of its turnover and ambiguity—serves a number of functions. It provides: (1) an additional device for recruiting clergymen, (2) a haven for clergymen too "radical" for the parish structure, (3) another means of alignment (along with seminaries) between church and intellectual centers, and (4) a means of routing innovation into the church via campus clergymen who return to the parish, students drawn into church life, and the leadership campus ministers can more readily give to "radical" causes, such as (in our day) civil-rights protests and the ecumenical movement.[1]

But as we have seen in foregoing chapters, campus ministers themselves, by a great majority, desire less ambiguity in their occupation; and denominations are hopeful that turnover can be reduced. Also, though it has been clear from the beginning of this analysis that "effectiveness" of the campus ministry is not to be equated with its institutionalization, we discovered a relationship between shared expectations and at least self-assigned effectiveness. It might be reasonable, then, to anticipate some improvement in the quality of ministries on campus should there be an increase in shared expectations and a reduction in turnover. Put in other words, though clearly an institutionalized role is not necessarily more effective, it is likely that some degree of institutionalization is a necessary precondition for effectiveness to be more than accidental. The instances of effective campus ministries, we are saying, have been accidents—the results of coincidental coming together of man, campus, and church.

Why is this so? Basically the answer, as we uncovered it in preceding chapters, is threefold. (1) Conditions have inhibited a shift from borrowed to indigenous expectations because of the constant challenge of historical developments in theology, seminary education, the church, and higher education. (2) Conditions have inhibited a shift from borrowed to indigenous commitment because some campus ministers have been committed to borrowed pastoral style, while others, though pursuing potentially indigenous, innovative styles, have been committed more to the "campus" than to the "ministry." And (3) social structural arrangements have been such that persons most likely to develop an indigenous commitment are least likely to be in positions marked by shared expectations. The analysis in Chapters 3 to 6 was geared to these possibilities; it drew from Chapter 2 a theoretical perspective which sees the path of institutionalization as a path whereby expectations become shared and commitment to them becomes indigenous.

In approaching the matter of compensatory policy changes, however, we find another theoretical perspective from Chapter 2 to be more useful. This is the perspective which sees the institutionalization of social behavior as surrounded by four conditions: recruitment, training, motivation, and adaptation. Most suggestions of how to "improve" the campus ministry are recommendations for altering one or more of these conditions. Thus, one denominational administrator said in an interview, when asked what contributed to a successful campus ministry: "The major issue here is not primarily the differences in circumstances on the campus but in the different ways by which persons approach the job." Others recommend that campus ministers have academic qualifications on a par with those of the faculty at their schools.[2] By implication, then, training is the major key to a more viable campus ministry.

Other observers would put the burden on the selection process. Finding "most able and prophetic men" or "the right kind of pastor" suggests that the recruitment condition could be better met. The denominational administrators (quoted in Chapter 6) who watch for campus ministers "escaping" from the church or "still playing college ball," along with those administrators who would improve sabbatical, insurance, and retirement provisions, are suggesting that changes in motivation will have a salutary effect.

Still others point to the condition of adaptation. Some years ago, for example, Shedd warned against trying to "combine the functions of a university pastor with those of a teacher of academic courses in religion" because they are "professional tasks with differing and exacting demands." [3] At a different level of analysis, a university administrator says, "The first thing I often wish for is that there might be less misunderstanding and mistrust between the church and the university." [4] In either case, the incompatibilities represent problems in adaptation—of people to their jobs or of church and university to each other.

The present research would suggest that none of these measures is likely to have much impact. Let us consider several in order to see why:

(1) Recruitment, generally speaking, is (or will be) no problem in the campus ministry. Because the number of persons wanting to be campus clergymen is much greater than the number of positions to be filled, considerable selectivity can occur. [5] The question, then, is the *basis* of the selectivity; what kinds of campus ministers would most likely facilitate institutionalization?

(2) Suppose denominations encouraged pastoral-style campus ministries. In effect, by doing away with special seminary curricula, internships, workshops, and so forth, and by promulgating a conception of the campus ministerial role as little different from that of its parish counterpart, denominations would encourage pastoral style. And pastoral style is met with greater acknowledgment. Would not the campus ministry be more likely to institutionalize if persons of a certain kind were recruited and they were trained in a certain way? The answer, of course, is that another source of innovative style—cosmopolitanism—would still be in force, constantly challenging the

"establishment" of pastoral style. Trying to restrict the campus ministry to persons and patterns of a certain kind is not likely, therefore, to be a solution. Developments in higher education will go on.

(3) Suppose, however, denominations encouraged innovative style. If they restricted recruitment and training to those persons and patterns likely to yield innovative style, would not the campus ministry be better able to institutionalize? Again the answer has to be no. For one thing, university acknowledgment is not contingent on style. And for another, denominational acknowledgment seems doomed to lag behind whatever innovation occurs in its midst. The history of the missionary movement at least would suggest this generality. The first Protestant missionary in the East, Bartholomew Ziegenbalg, would find much sympathy among today's innovative campus ministers. Arriving in South India in 1706, he saw that his first task was to assess the religious potential of his non-Christian audience.

> This sympathy found expression in a work of pioneer research, *The Genealogy of the South India Gods*. But Ziegenbalg was unable to communicate his own interests to the authorities . . . in Europe; on receipt of his manuscript, they dispatched to him the acid comment that his task was to proclaim the glorious Gospel to the heathen and not to propagate heathenish superstition in the West—and the book remained unpublished for a hundred and fifty years.[6]

From the rites controversy surrounding the Jesuits in seventeenth-century China or Church of England Bishop Copleston's tempest in the teapot of nineteenth-century Ceylon, down to present-day instances of worker-priests in France or the religio-psychiatric movement in America, the church has shown a remarkable capacity both to encourage innovation and then discourage it by failing to acknowledge it.[7] There is no reason to think the church will respond differently to the campus ministry.

(4) Suggestions have been made that certain "personality traits" may be better suited for the position of campus clergyman, and that selectivity according to such traits may yield a more viable occupation. There is no denying, of course, that at least gross personality characteristics can be in more or less harmony with gross characteristics of jobs. An "attractive personality, with health, humor, love of people, and friendliness," with "tact and ability to work with others," describes appropriate traits for almost any occupation, however, at least any involving interpersonal contact. Admonition that campus ministers be so selected, therefore, is gratuitous; the personality syndrome peculiarly appropriate for the campus ministry (if there is one [8]) must be more specific. Besides, institutionalization implies the substitutability of persons, the creation of a social structure into which many kinds of personality may fit. Restricting recruits to a certain type may solve some problems, but it does not solve the failure at institutionalization.[9]

(5) Still another "solution" recommended by some is, in effect, to do nothing. Some persons, perhaps characteristically in poorly institutionalized endeavors, insist that "every situation is different" and guidelines cannot be laid down.

> There are two things which need to be emphasized . . . each expression of the Church in the university, temporary or continuing, must discover for itself how to carry out its task as God's People. . . . [And second] the service which is to be given by the Church within the university is not of its own choosing but it is a service given unto it to perform by God.[10]

Apart from mixing theological with empirical analysis, such a statement pretends to helpfulness by providing no help at all. Each campus ministry cannot be left to "discover for itself" how to carry out its task. To make such a recommendation is to deny all that *is* known of the conditions of recruitment, training, motivation, and adaptation—conditions known to mold and modify various "expressions of the Church in the university." Indeed, as Niebuhr has stated, after a survey of historic instances of "definite, intelligible conceptions of the ministry":

> . . . a clear-cut conception always includes not only an understanding of what the most important work of the ministry is but also the recognition that it must perform other functions. Unity is given to such a conception [however] not only by ordering functions in a scale of importance but by directing each function to a chief, though still proximate, end.[11]

It may be that "the most important work" or "a chief, though still proximate, end" is not yet recognized in the campus ministry, but to assert that it cannot or must not be recognized is to lessen its chances of becoming so.

THE FUTURE OF THE CAMPUS MINISTRY

But has the analysis here not had the same result? Have we not observed the campus ministry to be set in a web of variables such that a change in one elicits contradicting changes in others? Are not the conditions of recruitment, training, motivation, and adaptation being met in such a manner that the role of campus clergyman is bound to remain poorly institutionalized?

The answer probably must be yes if the contemplated policy change would be only to select campus ministers with this or that role conception, or only to train them to this or that style, or only to "educate" church and university to emit this or that kind of acknowledgment.[12] A low level of institutionalization is likely to continue, in other words, if the attempt is to reverse the direction of change in theology, of developments in higher education, or of conservatism in denominations. These broad influences simply do not bend to fit their partial manifestations. Especially is this true when, as with the campus ministry, conflicting directions are manifested in the same pattern of activity.[13]

But the answer may be that the campus ministry is *not* bound to remain poorly institutionalized. If, instead of trying to reverse the direction of contextual changes, the campus ministry can fasten onto one and neutralize the others—if it can reflect the changes in the theological sphere but nullify the effects of low acknowledgment from church and university—then it may proceed to institutionalize. Such a procedure involves costs, perhaps more than would willingly be paid, but the procedure is possible. It has appeared over and over again in the occupational world. It is known as professionalization.

As members of the clergy, campus ministers already are professionals, of course, so by suggesting "professionalization" as a potential solution to the structural strains in their specialized occupation we do not mean to get embroiled in a logomachy. The definition of a profession is not uniform in the social sciences, and differences within the clergy or between the clergy and others are probably even less uniform.[14] Nevertheless, two core characteristics seem to stand out: (1) specialized training in some abstract body of knowledge, and (2) a service, or altruistic, orientation toward practice.[15] Professionalization of the campus ministry, beyond the degree to which it already shares these characteristics with the clergy generally, would involve, therefore, at least its *own* specialized training in its *own* abstract body of knowledge—apart from other clergy.

But more than this—professionalizing groups tend to take on some or all of the following characteristics:

(1) determination of their own standards of training;
(2) licensure requirement;
(3) manning of licensing boards by members of the profession;

(4) freedom from lay evaluation and control;
(5) strong identification and affiliation by members with each other;
(6) expectation that the profession is a terminal occupation.[16]

Professionalization of the campus ministry, then, not only means the development of special skills and special training, in some measure distinct from those of parish clergy, but also means that campus ministers will set their own standards, evaluate themselves, identify themselves as campus clergy, and view their occupation as a lifelong career. Whether one wants to call the result a separate profession, or a subprofession, or a structurally differentiated segment of an existing profession is immaterial. The fact is that a process involving some or all of the above characteristics could solve the campus ministry's problem of institutionalization. What is the prognosis?

Our discussion of borrowed and indigenous expectations and commitment in the campus ministry indicates the potentiality for professionalization. A sizable sector of present-day clergymen on campus have had specialized training and do have a differentiated conception of their role. They happen also to be more likely to conduct innovative (that is, differentiated) ministries. Moreover, they are more committed to the idea of a campus ministry. As incipient "professionals," therefore, they represent a core in the professionalization process. *This* aspect of the occupation need not change; it already has fastened onto theological changes going on around it. Problematic are *other* aspects: university and denominational acknowledgment. Since lack of acknowledgment now impedes institutionalization, but since acknowledgment is not amenable to manipulation, the question is whether the effects of its absence can be neutralized. Such neutralization is clearly one of the functions of professional associations.[17]

FACTORS UNFAVORABLE TO PROFESSIONALIZATION

Foremost of the problems is denominationalism. For the campus ministry to professionalize, *its* boundaries must take precedence over boundaries between denominations. To the degree that financial support, training, administration, and personnel are channeled through them, denominations have considerable claim on their campus ministries. Giving up any of that claim represents a change which may be difficult. Ecumenism has a certain foothold already, of course, and allowing higher-education units to be among the first to be "ecumenical" may be a logical step. The cooperation between denominations, and in some instances even the disappearance of ecclesiastical lines, in foreign missions is a precedent. But the change will be as difficult for churches as for others. Carr-Saunders has noted that: "When a new profession evolves within an existing profession . . . the practitioners of the new craft usually remain for a time in the shelter of their ancient home, and in consequence, the segregation of the new profession is delayed." [18] And Goode notes an additional likelihood:

> A sociological guess is that the most severe skirmishes . . . occur between the new profession and the occupations closest to it in substantive and clientele interest. . . . Moreover, practitioners within a field are not likely to be united among themselves; they will include some of the bitterest opponents of professionalization. [19]

A second barrier to professionalization, therefore, is seen in the meager proportion of campus ministers who recognize the structural importance to themselves of autonomy from church and college. They were asked: "Some campus clergy feel that the campus ministry would be more effective if it were less dependent on the institutional church for social, psychological, and financial help. Others feel that such autonomy would be detrimental. How do you feel?" The modal answer was, "The present situation generally is fine." Only 27 per cent indicated that they thought more autonomy would be beneficial, and about the same number (30 per cent) thought it would be detrimental. Comparable answers were given to an analogous question asked about autonomy from the college. Being now dependent in some measure on both church and college, present-day campus ministers hesitate to endorse greater autonomy for themselves.

These answers reflect in part a phenomenon not unique to campus ministers—that of professionals in bureaucracies: "The professional who is also a bureaucrat becomes less *directly* dependent on the professional community for his career advancement, so that the ordinary sanctions of that community may have less impact." [20] Campus ministers, being dependent on one or both bureaucracies surrounding them, are understandably wary of loosening those ties before a substitute looks likely.

Still another factor unfavorable to professionalization of the campus ministry is found in the nature of its present specialized training. A survey taken by a faculty member of one theological school revealed that the various programs around the country for training campus ministers contain minimal "professional orientation" or "professional methods" courses.[21] When such courses are virtually contentless, they are difficult to justify, even in the professional school curriculum. But their function is seldom restricted merely to transmission of techniques; perhaps more important is the conveying of values, the development of an occupational identity, which inculcates in trainees a sense of their endeavor's worth and uniqueness. To the degree these courses are missing from the campus ministerial curriculum, professionalization is impeded.

Factors Favorable to Professionalization

But a number of signs point to the possibility of professionalization. First in importance, perhaps, is the momentum already built up. As early as 1907, a "professionals' group" convened its first "Interdenominational Conference of Church and Guild Workers in State Universities," and in 1923 it expanded to include campus clergy at non-public schools.[22] It is instructive to note the interdenominational character of these early efforts and to note that "emphasis upon sectarianism" or any "attempt to build up the church as an end in itself" was anathema to some.[23] As the separate denominations were initiating their campus ministries and their separate associations of campus ministers, some sentiment, therefore, was also being expressed for a single professional group, one that would be ecumenical in membership if not in program.[24] Chaplains, as we mentioned in Chapter 1, have typically conducted their ministry through an interdenominational or nondenominational organization,[25] and their professional group (National Association of College and University Chaplains), with its annual convention and periodic journal, has flourished since its formation in 1947.

A second sign of latent professionalization of the campus ministry is seen in the favorable sentiments of its present practitioners. Almost all (86 per cent) think campus clergymen themselves are best able to develop and state a "code of ethics" or a "set of standards" for their occupation.[26] And a clear majority (61 per cent) choose campus clergy as the group "best able to evaluate" a campus minister. When, in another question, "faculty" was added to the list of possible answers, and respondents were asked to indicate the three groups "whose opinion of your ministry you consider the more important," "other campus ministers" led the balloting with 71 per cent. Ninety-three per cent would like to see "more specialized training given to those entering the campus ministry." [27] Of strategic importance is the set of answers given to a three-pronged question: "Would you like to see even stronger national and regional association, that is, more communication, more conventions, more members, made up of the following persons?" The answers are shown in Table 7–1.

TABLE 7–1.

	PER CENT FAVORING
Campus clergy in your own denomination	52
Campus clergy in many Protestant denominations	72
Campus clergy of Protestant, Catholic, and Jewish faiths	74

The potential support for more (especially non-denominational) organization is apparent.

In keeping with this implicit support of more profession-wide association is campus ministers' approval of an ecumenical campus ministry. They were asked if they favored "the merger of various denominational campus ministries on the same campus whenever possible." Almost half (42 per cent) said they would "very much" like such a move, and another quarter (28 per cent) would "like it somewhat." Fewer than a third, in other words, would not favor denominational merger at the campus ministry level.

Understandably, not all sentiment favors professionalization. Several aspects, at least, are not yet acceptable to a majority of campus ministers. Only a quarter (26 per cent) ranked as one of four "relatively more important" goals that of trying "to develop and articulate a theological basis for the campus ministry." It is a little difficult to see how the campus ministry, without such a theological base, can justify its existence as an occupation differentiated from other clergy.

And only a third (35 per cent) agree that the campus ministry should be its own personnel bureau, "so that notice of job openings and new positions and the movement of persons from job to job are done independently of the churches." Again, unless movement and advancement of personnel are under the control of campus clergy themselves, then setting their own standards and evaluating each other (two of the major functions of professional association) would seem to go for nought.

On the other hand, of specific significance is the fact that these sentiments favoring professionalization are more characteristic of "core" campus ministers (those with innovative style and predisposed to remain in the occupation, that is, those most likely to shift from borrowed to indigenous expectations and commitment). Also strategic is the fact that where campus ministers have the opportunity to join with others of like situation, they tend to do so. Seventy-one per cent have "regularly scheduled meetings more than once a year with campus ministers from other campuses." Of the 80 per cent on campuses with more than one campus clergyman, 53 per cent have "formal or informal contact" with each other at least several times weekly. Moreover, 29 per cent of campus ministers on these multistaff campuses have developed a plan "whereby each takes responsibility for some special type of ministry," which nine times out of ten involves two or more denominations.

And then there are the uniting professional efforts already in existence. In 1960, four denominations merged their student associations into one movement known as the United Campus Christian Fellowship.[28] What was easier to begin at the student level developed five years later, at the occupational level, into a National Campus Ministry Association. Furthermore, to the original four (Disciples, United, Evangelical and United Brethren, and Presbyterian, U.S.A.) has been added a fifth (Moravian). In the process, each denomination disbanded its own campus ministerial association and invited any denomination "willing to accept the constitution and designate this association as *its* association" to join also. Conversations, and presumably negotiations, are under way with American Baptists, Methodists, Lutherans, and Episcopalians. The constitution [29] is interesting. It states that the purposes of the association include:

(1) foster the educational development of its members;
(2) facilitate approaches with other individuals and agencies of the church to ministry and mission in higher education;
(3) listen to and speak to the church and to the university on these matters;
(4) advance ecumenical understanding;
(5) provide a supportive fellowship for its members.

The significance of such a professional association remains to be seen. One of the member denominations hopes it will "stimulate writing for learned journals," "encourage the writing and publishing of books in higher education," and develop a "philosophy and pattern of continuing education for the campus ministry." Along with "supportive fellowship," these sound like the characteristics of a differentiating profession. But whether this sound is merely the rhetoric of professionalization or represents truly its substance is contingent on much more than the appearance of a constitution. Will university pastors, of which this latter group is composed, join with chaplains and *their* association? Will some denominations hold back from full support? Will it be necessary or possible to include non-Protestant campus clergy? Will churches be willing to relinquish some of their present control over personnel, promotion, and program?

It will be noted that these questions are asked of the church and not of the university. The reason is quite simple: The object of professionalization is not to increase the acknowledgment of either sphere—to which the campus ministry is presently vulnerable—but to neutralize the effects of low acknowledgment. Professionalization, by whatever name it is called, is the task of those who most desire a campus ministry. Changes, then, are left to the denominations and campus clergy themselves.

CONCLUSION

Should many of these changes be possible, greater institutionalization of the campus ministry can be anticipated. One result will, of course, be loss of flexibility. With specific standards, set and administered by the campus ministry itself, not only will individual persons and denominations have less freedom in appointments and promotion, but also there will be more limitation on programming. What is a decrease in ambiguity is an increase in limitation. With the campus ministry a terminal occupation, denominations will lose some power to move persons in and out of positions. What is an increase in commitment or a decrease in turnover is a loss of freedom in personnel allocation. With growing identification and affiliation of campus ministers with each other, denominational boundaries will recede in importance. What is institutionalization of the campus ministry is, in some measure, therefore, a decrease in denominational integrity.

These costs may be considered excessive by some. It has not been the task of this analysis to arrive at *the* answer. Rather, we have demonstrated the inefficacy of possible other policy changes and pointed to the viability of another—professionalization. Perhaps the costs of this one measure are greater than its reward, but if the purchase is made, we have little doubt about its delivery: increased institutionalization of the campus ministry.

NOTES

1. For elaboration on these points, see Hammond and Mitchell, *op. cit.*
2. For example, see Erich A. Walter, "For Governing Boards and University Administrators," *Journal of Higher Education,* XXX (1959), 215.
3. Shedd, *op. cit.,* p. 286.
4. Harold K. Schilling, "The University and the Church," lectures given at the Annual Meeting of the Fellowship of Campus Ministry (of the Congregational Christian Church and the Evangelical and Reformed Church), June, 1955. Privately printed.
5. See above, p. 41. This statement may not be applicable to the same degree in every denomination.
6. Neill, *op. cit.,* pp. 9–10. See also the account of Ziegenbalg in Neill's *A History of Christian Missions* (Harmondsworth, Middlesex, U.K.: Penguin Books, 1964), pp. 228–231.
7. A considerable literature exists on the rites controversy. The standard work is K. S. Latourette, *A History of Christian Missions in China* (New York: Macmillan, 1929), though A. H. Rowbotham, *Missionary and Mandarin: The Jesuits at the Court of China* (Berkeley and Los Angeles: University of California Press, 1942) is a fuller treatment. Neill, *op. cit.,* p. 513, discusses Bishop Copleston. *The Worker-Priests: A Collective Documentation,* trans. John Petrie (London: Routledge and Kegan Paul, 1956) contains many documents on the rise and fall of this ministry to laborers. See also William Bosworth, *Catholicism and Crisis in Modern France* (Princeton: Princeton University Press, 1962). The Vatican Council has, of course, led to the reinstitution of the movement, though with restrictions. Samuel Z. Klausner, *Psychiatry and Religion* (New York: Free Press of Glencoe, 1964) discusses the development of the religio-psychiatric movement. See especially his pertinent comments on its institutionalization in "The Religio-Psychiatric Movement," *Review of Religious Research,* V–VI (1964), 63–74, 7–22.
8. In one instance known to the writer, research was conducted to discover personality differences between campus clergy and ex-campus clergy. Twenty dimensions or traits were in-

vestigated. One out of those 20 revealed a difference at the .05 level of significance, about the number expected by chance.

9. In their paper, "From Evangelism to General Service: The Transformation of the YMCA," *Administrative Science Quarterly*, VIII (1963), 214–234, M. N. Zald and P. Denton raise the question of how the YMCA was able to undergo major change in goals, organization, and activity without disintegrating. In effect, their answer is because the YMCA was not highly institutionalized. *One* of the pieces of evidence is their discovery that the personality of the Y secretary tends to be peculiarly suited to the activities toward which the YMCA is moving. In other words, transformation may be facilitated by recruiting a personality "type," but institutionalization may not.

10. Duley, *op. cit.*, p. 22.

11. H. Richard Niebuhr (with D. D. Williams and J. M. Gustafson), *The Purpose of the Church and Its Ministry* (New York: Harper and Bros., 1956), pp. 62–63.

12. There is a possible exception to this generality regarding the futility of making "single" changes, only to have them contradicted by other variables in the system. Recruitment procedures could eliminate in advance those persons who, though predisposed to indigenous expectations, are also committed more to the campus than to the campus ministry—the would-be teachers discussed in the previous chapter.

13. In this sense, the campus ministry *is* one arena for conflict between religion and higher education. Contrary to initial expectation, however, such conflict is not expressed as *role* conflict in the campus ministry because of its low level of institutionalization. See Chapter 6.

14. M. L. Cogan, "Toward a Definition of Profession," *Harvard Educational Review*, XXIII (1953), 33–50, is a 17-page survey of various definitions. H. L. Wilensky, "The Professionalization of Everyone?" *American Journal of Sociology*, LXX (1964), 137–158, is a healthy reminder not to mistake the "rhetoric of professionalism" for its substance.

15. See, e.g., William J. Goode, "Encroachment, Charlatanism, and the Emerging Profession," *American Sociological Review*, XXV (1960), 903; Talcott Parsons, *Essays in Sociological Theory* (Glencoe, Ill.: The Free Press, 1954), p. 372.

16. These are taken from a longer list in Goode, *op. cit.*, p. 903.
17. "Indeed, the professional group requires control over its members precisely *because* its judgments do not coincide generally with those of clients. As a consequence, its members *need* the protection of the professional community and submit to its demands." William J. Goode, "Community within a Community: The Professions," *American Sociological Review*, XXII (1957), 197. (Italics in the original.)
18. A. M. Carr-Saunders and P. A. Wilson, *The Professions* (Oxford: Clarendon Press, 1933), p. 298.
19. Goode, "Encroachment, Charlatanism, and the Emerging Profession," pp. 903–904.
20. Goode, "Community within a Community: The Professions," p. 197. (Italics in the original.) On this matter for clergy generally, see Joseph Fichter, S.J., *Religion as an Occupation* (South Bend, Ind.: University of Notre Dame Press, 1960).
21. Private communication with Prof. J. Edward Dirks of the Yale Divinity School.
22. Shedd, *op. cit.*, p. 72.
23. *Loc. cit.*
24. The roots of present-day ecumenism in the religion-and-higher-education movement are clear. See, e.g., R. S. Bilheimer, *The Quest for Christian Unity* (New York: Association Press, 1952), pp. 81–82; R. Rouse and S. Neill (eds.), *A History of the Ecumenical Movement* (Philadelphia: Westminster Press, 1954), p. 341.
25. ". . . only a very few [4 of 150] considered denominational groups a major channel for their work." Seymour A. Smith, *The American College Chaplaincy*, p. 85.
26. Other choices: teachers of theology, denominational officials, college administrators, parish ministers.
27. The National Council of Churches is beginning a New Staff Seminar for campus ministers, presumably for a few weeks prior to their first campus job. At present, eight member denominations of the National Council are involved.
28. For particulars, see V. L. Barker, "The United Campus Christian Fellowship" in Earnshaw (ed.), *The Campus Ministry*, pp. 277–299.
29. At this writing, only mimeographed copies have been available.

APPENDIX

A NATURAL HISTORY OF THE RESEARCH

It was during a chance conversation in the spring of 1960 that Dr. Yoshio Fukuyama alerted me to the possibility of studying the campus ministry. He is the Director of Research for the United Church of Christ, and had just been contacted by one of the state organizations of campus ministers in that denomination. They wanted to know if research could be undertaken to help them better define their task as campus ministers. Fukuyama did indeed help conduct some interviews, identify some problematic areas, and make some recommendations. But as he noted from the beginning, this was but one denomination, in one small geographic area, and involved only university pastors, not chaplains. Are problems of ambiguity endemic to the campus ministry, he wondered out loud to me, and if so, why?

I was in the process of moving from Columbia University, where I was a graduate student, to Yale University to assume my first full-time teaching position. With new surroundings, new course preparations, and so forth, I put little thought to the campus ministry for almost a year. The exceptions occurred as I got to know Parker Rossman and J. Edward Dirks of Yale Divinity School, the men who taught courses in religion and higher education—the specialty training courses for campus ministers. From them I heard that campus clergymen generally were beset with the problems of which Fukuyama had spoken. I also learned that a growing literature was available on the campus ministry, that chaplains had formed a professional association which met in convention annually, and that very little systematic information about the campus ministry really existed. For example, no one really knew how many practitioners the occupation had. Despite denominational rosters, there was no clear distinction among full-time campus clergymen, assistant ministers of college-town churches whose primary responsibility might be college personnel or might be Christian education generally, parish clergy who might drive over to a campus for counseling hours one afternoon a week, and women volunteers who kept the coffeepot boiling in the foundation house.

During the spring of 1961, therefore, I undertook two things. First, I began to read some literature by and about campus ministers—denominational statements, descriptions of programs, debates over aims, and so forth, as well as books and articles. The theme of ambiguity certainly came through in this reading, and I was developing more and more interest in the prospective research. The second thing, therefore, was to write the Danforth Foundation about possible funding. Concerned with religion in higher education, they were, I was told, the logical place to turn.

Their reply was peculiar. They were not then prepared, they said, to support my empirical research, but they were convinced of the need for large amounts of information, speculation, philosophical analysis, and pragmatic recommendations in the area of the campus ministry. Would I, therefore, attend a conference in the summer at which a major research program might be planned? I would, and I did, hoping that an immediate consequence would be funds for conducting my own research.

That hope was unrealistic. The eventual outcome of the conference was creation of The Danforth Foundation Commission for the Study of Campus Ministries, and, as it turned out, most of my support came from this commission. But this was to be later. Meanwhile, I was impatient to start, so in the fall of 1961 I turned to the National Institute of Mental Health. One category of application is called "Small Grant," a category for putting up to $3,500 into the hands of young researchers or those who needed funds for preliminary stages of projects. I qualified on both counts, and an award was given. To extend from April, 1962, for about a year, this grant allowed me to travel around the Eastern seaboard, recording interviews with campus ministers and other relevant persons. It also paid for getting transcripts of those interviews, excerpts of which are interspersed throughout this book, and it helped pay for the questionnaires.

I could not interview any representative sample, of course, but I did try to talk with university pastors and chaplains, from various denominations, in large and small, and public and private colleges. I interviewed from Massachusetts to Virginia, and I spoke not only to campus ministers but also to denominational administrators, a few college administrators, and even an interested faculty member at one school. By attending an annual convention of the National Association of College and University Chaplains, I was also able to interview chaplains, if not university pastors, from the South, West, and Midwest. All told, I ended with 20 formal interviews, plus notes from informal contacts or chance conversations.

Throughout this period, I continued to read. That reading, plus the general drift of the interviews, convinced me that the most likely approach to my study would be by way of the notion of conflict. Sir Walter Moberly (*The Crisis in the University*) and Alexander Miller (*Faith and Learning*), for example, implied that the religious and educational institutions are, in some senses, at odds with each other. Organized differently, and promulgating different values, the church and college at times conflict. Would not the campus ministry be caught, then, in the middle? Would not role conflict be the conceptual tool for explaining the ambiguity?

I certainly thought so, and memoranda to myself and others at this time discussed the research strategy necessary for documentation and interpretation. As Chapter 6 makes clear, this was an inaccurate estimate, but apart from information lost that would have been available had some other questions been used, no great harm was done. Such, incidentally, is one of the advantages of the broad-gauged approach in survey research. Sensitivity to events in interviews will likely lead to relevant areas of questions even if the explicit rationale is not wholly accurate. Thus, for example, the questions regarding how well various persons in college and church *know* the respondent's work were asked chiefly to introduce the next set of questions: Do those persons *approve* or *disapprove* of that work? Obviously, I was interested in the relationship between knowledge and approval, but what I did not anticipate was the virtual absence of disapproval. This meant that "knowledge" questions, not "approval" questions, had to be the major linkage between campus ministers and their dual "audiences." But, fortunately, the questions were asked, presumably because the initial interviewing sensitized me to the *general* problem of responses to campus ministers by college and church.

In the summer of 1962, the Danforth Foundation had not yet formally committed funds for the broad program their Commission was eventually to undertake. However, I still had some of the N.I.M.H. Small Grant, and correspondence with Danforth suggested that their Board would approve funds for a Commission (they did in November, 1962), part of which might trickle to me. So, I went ahead on two fronts: designing a questionnaire and writing to denominations for their campus ministry rosters of names and addresses.

Late that summer, the campus ministers of several denominations were holding their annual conferences simultaneously at Beloit College. I drafted a questionnaire and flew out to Wisconsin with 100 or so copies, hoping to pretest the adequacy of my instrument and try some preliminary analysis. Conditions were not good, however. I could elicit no "sponsorship" from the officers of the conference, and I went away with fewer than two dozen completed questionnaires. These, of course, were helpful in spotting badly worded items, items with insufficient alternative answers, and so forth. More importantly, perhaps, I came to realize campus ministers' antipathy toward questionnaires. They are inundated, it seems, by requests from seminary students or thesis writers. One outcome for me, then, was to plan a questionnaire and its distribution so as to neutralize this antipathy.

On the basis of the first draft, I wrote another questionnaire —this one pretested with the Protestant campus ministers at Yale—and still another, answered by several of the persons I had previously interviewed. I promised "immunity" from the final product to these two groups, incidentally, and so they are not included in the data reported in the book.

I was also, during this time, developing a master list of campus ministers. Parker Rossman's office regularly collects the rosters of the denominations having enough campus ministers to warrant some special administrative attention (there were 11 of these in 1963), and I simply wrote for these lists, added the membership of the national chaplains' association, and eliminated duplications. Some campus clergymen no doubt escaped this net. In addition to the dozen or so promised immunity for cooperating with pretests, there may be some isolated instances of overlooked persons. Overlooked, for example, might be chaplains who are neither members of the chaplains' association nor listed by their denominations as campus ministers, and campus ministers in those denominations which prepare no roster. Both categories, I had good reason to believe, are very small, since I found some chaplains who were not members of N.A.C.U.C. but were listed by denominations, and I did have the roster of the Evangelical and United Brethren Church, a roster which added only three names not elsewhere listed. Denominations without rosters, I reasoned, would supply even fewer additional names.

The final questionnaire was printed by the Yale University Press in March 1963. Prior to sending it out, however, I had a letter printed on Yale Divinity School letterhead and signed by Professors J. Edward Dirks and James Gustafson, persons whom most recipients were likely to know and recognize as theologians. This initial contact went out to the approximately 1,600 names on the master list with a request for cooperation and for notification from anyone no longer a campus minister or mistakenly appearing on the list. In April 1963, the questionnaire was sent to 1,514 persons, some 85 having signified their "ineligibility."

I shall return to the matter of response rates to the questionnaire, but first we must back up in order to describe some other decisions that were made.

From the beginning, I had assumed that the research would involve only full-time or nearly full-time campus ministers. The decision to restrict it to Protestants came from the obvious fact that inclusion of Catholics and Jews would necessitate different questionnaires, thus reducing points of comparison. Moreover, if major differences existed among the three groups (as I suspected), then one would have to analyze them separately anyway. I was operating on a further assumption—that estimates I had heard of three to four thousand Protestant campus clergy were estimates of full-time people. The rosters of names were enough to correct that impression, however, since they clearly included parish ministers of churches in college towns, assistant ministers whose various duties included academic populations, and so forth. Instead of sampling from a longer list, therefore, I could now take the universe of the shorter list, having written to the denominations not only for permission to poll their campus ministers, but also to verify that I was correctly reading the roster nomenclature.

I further decided to ask more detailed "filter" questions, items regarding any non-campus work engaged in, and what percentage of time was given to campus work. As we shall see, another group of respondents were disqualified on the basis of their answers to these questions.

Throughout this period, and for another year, money remained a problem. Because I had gone ahead with my own work, the Danforth Commission never really considered my work, nor did I consider it, part of "their" program, though they (through the person of its Director, Kenneth W. Underwood) let it be known that work would not have to stop. Consequently, for example, they gave me $1,000 to help pay for printing the questionnaire, stamps, clerical assistance in addressing, and so forth. Together with the residue of N.I.M.H.'s Small Grant, this money almost got the data collected. The Department of Sociology at Yale picked up the tab for the remaining $375.

But this was just to collect the data. Coding, punching, and analysis still remained. Then, too, I was hoping for a year's leave in order to complete the analysis and write the results. I therefore tried several other sources of funds. The private foundations I contacted, though interested in religion and higher education, could not or would not believe that social research in the area was worth supporting. The federal agencies I contacted, though interested in occupational problems and stress, could not or would not believe that the Protestant campus ministry was a relevant locus of investigation. Indeed, one of them hinted that the addition of Catholics and Jews would have made it easier to grant federal money.

Such was my position in the summer of 1963. Having begun with long-range plans, carefully detailed budget, and expectations of completion in a reasonable time, I now found myself with a batch of completed questionnaires and no way to proceed. Again, however, the Danforth Commission came through, sending me this time $2,883, enough to complete the technical phases of the study. With this money I was able to hire four coders, have IBM cards punched, and pay some

Computer Center costs. Later still, the Commission paid my year's salary for 1964–65, but this gets us ahead of our story.

The initial letter and the appeal on the questionnaire itself resulted in a return rate of over 50 per cent. After seven weeks, I sent another letter, this one drafted and signed by Kenneth Underwood, to those persons who had not yet responded. An additional 9 per cent answered. After three more weeks, I sent another letter and received still another 8 per cent. And finally, after a month, I sent second copies of the questionnaire. By now it was the end of July, so when 9 per cent more came in by mid-September, I decided to close off the data collection. Inevitably, and as much as a year later, an occasional questionnaire would trickle in, but these were not used in the analysis.

Of the original 1,514 questionnaires sent in April, 82 per cent were accounted for, but 151 of these came back with notes that the recipients, through death, moves, retirement, or mistake, were not practicing campus ministers. These were classified as "disqualified," as were 100 others who returned questionnaires but who indicated, via filter questions, that they were involved in campus work less than half time. From the original master list of about 1,600, then, we had narrowed the "universe" of full-time or nearly full-time campus ministers to 1,263. Of these, 79 per cent (997) returned completed questionnaires, 21 per cent (260) were not heard from before the September deadline, and six persons refused to cooperate.

A response rate as high as 79 per cent is usually not achieved unless one has a select audience, motivated to respond. To a large extent, this is the case with campus ministers. Questions about their occupation, after all, are interesting to them. But in addition, several other techniques probably helped increase the response. First, of course, were the letters, not only from me but also from others whose names likely were known to respondents and whose "purity of motives" they could assume. Second, the questionnaire was designed to make answering easy. Almost all questions required only a check mark to answer, and aesthetically the instrument was appealing. Not dittoed or mimeographed, it was commercially printed, with the result that items were not cluttered on a page, every word was easily read, and so on. The rather high cost for such a job is probably worth paying, at least whenever the sample population is bombarded with questionnaires. Third, great care was taken to avoid offensive questions. As clergy, these respondents are used to being asked such items as "Do you believe in Heaven and Hell?" For persons whose occupation involves rather fine terminological distinctions in precisely those areas, such questions can be frustrating. So not only did I use qualifications and "softening" techniques to introduce many questions, but also I invited as many qualifications in the margins as the respondent chose to make. Coders were then instructed to take account of marginal comments in their coding.

Finally, some purely technical details probably helped increase the response. The questionnaire was sent in an envelope, but to return it in the mail one had only to fold over a flap and moisten one edge. And instead of an addressee-will-pay-upon-receipt symbol in the upper right corner, we went to the trouble of pasting a real postage stamp, hoping that the puritan strand in any clergyman would make him hesitate to throw away 15 cents.

Whatever the mixture of various motives, however, a 79 per cent return is quite high and probably can be trusted. We did check against return bias, though, in two standard ways. (Here "we" is literal; Frank Pokrass, a graduate student in one of my classes at the time, wrote a term paper in which he analyzed the data on which the following is based.) First, because the return date of the questionnaire was coded, the early and late returns could be compared. Dividing the 997 into seven categories ranging from earliest returns to latest returns, we found no differences in such items as how long respondents had been campus ministers, whether they had non-campus ministerial duties, whom they depended upon for salary and program planning, whether they felt their positions were vaguely defined, and so on. In other words, on a variety of items, early and late returnees were much alike. We might infer that non-returnees do not bias the sample if we make the following assumption: As late returnees differ from early returnees so do those who never responded differ from those who did respond.

We had access to some information about non-returnees, however. For all we had name (and thus sex) and address (and thus region) and for almost all we had denomination, whether chaplain or university pastor, and some information about the schools to which they ministered (such as size, coed or not, public or private, and church affiliation if private). Comparison on all these items did reveal a slight bias in the returns: There is some underrepresentation of Southern Baptist, female chaplains in small, private institutions in the South. Inspection indicates that this discrepancy could be accounted for by the Southern Baptist practice of including on their campus ministry roster a number of "chaplains" assigned to nursing schools attached to hospitals. Assuming that a high proportion of non-returnees are women who saw that the questionnaire did not really apply to hospitals, and assuming further that they did not notify me of their disqualification, then the underrepresentation is seen to be no bias at all. I cannot unequivically assert this to be the explanation, because the Southern Baptist list typically contained only names and street addresses, not school affiliations. But many signs point to it. If true, we can assume that the 79 per cent who did return questionnaires are representative of all Protestant campus ministers. The one exception is the fact noted in Chapter 1— the non-returnees had a higher turnover rate in 1963–64. Their greater likelihood of quitting, in other words, was further indicated in their apathy about responding.

Another source of bias in survey research comes at the coding stage; coders may err in transcribing questionnaire responses to code sheets. I tried to reduce this source of error in two ways. First, the instrument was "precoded," that is, every question was already assigned a column on an IBM card, and every possible answer assigned a punch in that column. Second, the coders were paid a base rate but promised bonus pay on the basis of the quality of their work. I randomly selected every tenth questionnaire they coded and recoded it. Since there was virtually no room for judgmental error to creep in, the errors I discovered were those of carelessness, and thus random. Needless to say, these were minimal; given 339 opportunities to err with each questionnaire, the coders averaged less than two careless mistakes. They all received bonus pay.

Still another source of error comes in punching the cards. Operators of the key punch can make mistakes as easily as typists. One way to catch such errors is to punch duplicate cards, assuming that random mistakes are highly unlikely to occur at the same place in both IBM cards. The duplicate cards can then be compared electronically, and disagreements corrected by the code sheets. Another way to catch punching errors is to "clean" the cards—running them through machines to note any punches that appear where they ought not to.

By November 1963, these various stages had been completed, and the analysis could begin. All the preceding chapters convey the outcome, of course, but one deviation only alluded to in Chapter 6 can profitably be pointed up here because, I suspect, it is fairly common, and certainly disconcerting.

Being confronted with 339 observations on 997 persons can be something like trying to find sequences in a table of random numbers. To avoid the inevitable frustration of that prospect, survey researchers routinely have a planned strategy for beginning the analysis. Mine, as I mentioned above, was the strategy of conflict, and the questionnaire contained many items to measure its nature and intensity. Conflict was to be a guiding theme in the eventual report.

One can imagine the horror, then, of discovering that those scoring "high" on measures of conflict were no more unhappy, dissatisfied, vague, or likely to quit than those scoring "low." Many other tables "made sense"; I was developing great confidence in the data; but obviously conflict (at least as I had conceived it) was not the key to understanding the campus ministry occupation. At this point, the only solution was to think up alternative explanatory "keys." The one I eventually settled upon came in the spring of 1964 when I chanced upon a new book in a colleague's office. The book is William A. Rushing, *The Psychiatric Professions*, a theoretical analysis of structural devices used by paramedical professions which are trying to gain greater attention and deference, and be of greater service, in the mental hospital. The points of similarity between those occupations and the campus ministry struck me. My analysis techniques and concepts were going to be different from Rushing's, but I was now led to ask entirely new questions of my data. If conflict was "absent," for example, might that indicate the fact that nobody "cares"? And could not the perception that nobody cares generate in campus ministers the same responses I noted before but had assumed to be consequences of conflict? Such, of course, is the way things turned out many months later, but it is instructive to see that most of my study was not overhauled. I went ahead with measures of campus ministry values, of campus ministerial styles, of college campus characteristics. But until the guiding theme was identified, these were but interesting classifications. The final scheme, as I recall it, came about in December 1964 and was contained chiefly in a chart that resembles Figure 6–1 in this book.

Another happy coincidence also occurred. After being notified by Underwood that I would be supported in a year's leave of absence, I made plans to spend the year at the University of California. Probably because I was in Berkeley, therefore, I was led to read the books of Burton R. Clark. I suppose I had known them before, but not until the fall of 1964 did their great relevance for my work become clear. For they, too, were analyses of poorly institutionalized social structures. The fact that Clark is at the University of California, and that we had several conversations about higher education and the campus ministry, meant, no doubt, that these analyses had greater impact on me than they otherwise would.

The guiding theme, or "plot," was thus determined. The second half of the year was spent developing that theme and drafting chapters. By the end of the leave period I was essentially finished, but because I had accepted an offer to move to the University of Wisconsin, and this meant delays, new course preparations, and so on, it was another half year before *The Campus Clergyman* finally went to press.

Aside from the distinct luxury of a year off from teaching duties, the budget for this project was very modest. Except for my salary for one calendar year, the total budget was a mere $6,133. Researchers infrequently report the itemized costs of their research, but because such information may be helpful to others contemplating work of similar scope, I conclude with figures on major expenditures.

(1) 2,000 copies of a 15-page questionnaire, plus covers and envelopes	$1,367
(2) Postage for questionnaires and follow-up letters	580
(3) Research assistance (chiefly coding)	1,215
(4) IBM machine costs (including punching cards)	450
(5) Clerical (chiefly typing addresses, transcribing interviews)	1,000

The remaining sum of about $1,500 went for travel, tape recorder, books, telephone tolls, and paper supplies. Most projects would have much higher expenses for machine costs, but I had free access to machines both at the Department of Sociology at Yale and at the Survey Research Center in Berkeley.

Clearly, no one volume can utilize all the information contained in lengthy questionnaires from almost 1,000 persons. For all of the questions asked and for the exact wording of items discussed in this volume, see Document 8814, deposited with the ADI Auxiliary Publications Project, Photoduplication Service, Library of Congress, Washington, D.C., 20540. A copy may be obtained by citing the Document number and by remitting $2.50 for photoprints, or $1.75 for 35 mm. microfilm. Advance payment is required. Make checks payable to Chief, Photoduplication Service, Library of Congress.

INDEX

167